THE ENLIGHTENED SMOKER'S GUIDE TO QUITTING

Bear Jack Gebhardt

Founder of The Smoker's Freedom School

BENBELLA

BENBELLA BOOKS, INC.
Dallas, Texas

BenBella Books, Inc.
6440 N. Central Expressway, Suite 503
Dallas, TX 75206
www.benbellabooks.com
Send feedback to feedback@benbellabooks.com

Printed in the United States of America
10 9 8 7 6 5 4 3 2 1

Library of Congress Cataloging-in-Publication Data is available for this title.

ISBN 193377137-2

Text design by Vernon Press, Inc., Boston, MA
Composition by CompuDesign, Jackson Heights, NY
Front matter design by Laura Watkins
Cover design by Laura Watkins

Distributed by Independent Publishers Group
To order call (800) 888-4741
www.ipgbook.com

For special sales contact Robyn White at robyn@benbellabooks.com

Dedication

This book is for Mom and Bob and Jim and Ornella, and all the rest of my smoking family—Mollie, Bobbie, George, Richard, Stephen, Pat, Wally, Jane, Panda, Vleska, and all the other of my smoking moms, dads, brothers, sisters, kids, near and far.

It's crazy, isn't it, this smoking life of ours? I love you guys. Hope this sets you freely grinning.

Acknowledgments

Thanks to Roberta Scimone at Element Books for seeing the potential in, and taking a chance on, this book. And to Brian Hotchkiss and his people at Vernon Press for their careful attention and happy insights. Their work made this book much better than it would have been otherwise.

Special thanks to Christian Almayrac, teacher and friend. And to Rebecca Mann, Stephen Johnson, Ted Gould, and Dana McBride for helping my practice with their practice. And to Annalee Gebhardt, my enlightened friend, walking-buddha buddy. And to Sam Gebhardt, a happy Christian man.

And most especially, my thanks and eternal devotion to Suzanne Summers Gebhardt—wife, companion, friend, bringer of happiness and light to my every hour. Without her healing joy and daily support, this book would not have been.

Contents

Introduction

If you want to use this book to quit smoking, you can. But you aren't *obliged* to use it for that purpose. In fact, you'll find this book to be the least critical about smoking of any book you'll ever read on the subject.

But if you want to use the book to help you stop smoking, at your own pace, in your own time, it has everything you'll need. You will be shown how to take tiny baby steps, so you will suffer no withdrawals, no miserable days. But it also shows you how to do it quick, split—right now, if you want—and maybe still have no withdrawals. Or you can use the book just to help you think about smoking a little more deeply, clearly, in an easy, no-pressure way.

However you decide to use the material in this book, you best hold onto your hat, friend, because your smoking life is about to leave the launching pad. What you are about to read is different from and, I promise, more radical than any other book you've ever read on the subject. (I think I've read them all.)

Fortunately, you don't have to decide right now just how you want to quit—quickly, slowly, or never. You just have to glimpse that this little adventure might be worth your while. It just might be what the doctor would order, if the doctor were enlightened about such things.

But first, you're probably wondering who is going to be your guide on this adventure. My name is Jack Gebhardt, and I'm founder of The Smoker's Freedom School. I had my first cigarette at age seven and my last smoke a little over three years ago when an old friend and I conducted a private Native American ceremony, which included smoking tobacco, for his old dog Rufus, who had recently departed. So, although I still feel free to *use* tobacco whenever I am so moved (very, very rarely), I have not been *addicted* to tobacco for over fifteen years. For the twenty years prior to that, I was, indeed, addicted.

For nine years during the 1970s, as an alternative to fighting in Vietnam, I worked for a drug education and treatment center, where we worked with street freaks, Vietnam vets, drug addicts, and curious kids who were just experimenting. I taught drug education classes at all grade levels and in college. My training in drug education and treatment was by some of the top people in the United States, including doctors and others from the Menninger Clinic in Topeka, Kansas; the Haight-Ashbury Free Clinic in San Francisco; local, state, and federal health agencies; the United States Department of Probation and Parole, and numerous other institutions. During all this time, working with "druggies" and teaching kids not to get addicted, I continued to smoke a pack to a pack and a half a day, which seemed a little weird.

I burned out on the drug education and training business, moved over to the other side of the rainbow and became a stockbroker with an international clientele, a three-piece suit and a Mercedes. After seven years of that life, I'd had enough, but in the meantime I'd found the mental and emotional energy I needed to quit my lifelong tobacco habit. I thought it was odd that I was finally able to quit only when I was making a lot of money, feeling good about my life, and wanting to feel still better. I grew extremely curious as to how I was able to quit in the middle of such a high-pressured, consistently uncertain work environment, and yet was *unable* to quit in the supportive, highly knowledgeable drug education and treatment environment.

So I read more about tobacco addiction and began to

research tobacco-treatment modalities and look at the problem, not only from the "professional" point of view, but also from my wider, more immediate life experiences. I made notes, wrote articles and essays, and started a book called *How to Stop Smoking in Fifteen Easy Years*.

Although I had become thoroughly conversant with the theories and practices of the stop-smoking industry, I still didn't feel that I had found the real secret to the whole smoking phenomenon—why we get started in the first place, why we continue for so long, why it is so hard to stop, and how and why eventually we do succeed.

I don't, as you'll read in this book, put all the blame on the chemical properties of nicotine. We make a mistake when we focus our attention there. My basic sense now is that nicotine is in fact a fairly mild drug—what has been called a "middle-class drug." It doesn't make the top of your head blow off, or send you into ecstasy, or boggle your mind, or make you as mellow as a log, like speed or cocaine or LSD or heroin. The addiction to nicotine may be as intense, but the effects are not. So why is it such a widespread indulgence, and, for many smokers, such a lifelong problem? I had the facts and figures, the theories and personal experiences, but still I didn't feel I had the key, the secret.

Then, early in 1993, I attended a lecture by a French physician, Christian Almayrac, who was billed as "Dr. Happiness." Listening to him speak, I realized that he probably had the key to the whole phenomenon. I arranged a private meeting with him and asked whether he had any experience with treating smokers.

"Oh yes, many of my patients have quit smoking," he said. "But that was not the intent. That was an accident, the by-product. Many just forgot to smoke!"

Forgot to smoke! I loved it. I had to find out how he did it—how *they* did it. For the next several years I studied intensively with Dr. Almayrac and applied what he taught to what I knew and to what my research had told me about stopping smoking. I tried out what I had learned on a small class of seven people. *Everybody quit!* I was pleasantly dumbfounded. The Smoker's Freedom School was launched.

I've taught stop-smoking classes at our local university, for major corporations, in private classes, at churches, and one-on-one. When it comes to tobacco, I'm an old warrior. I love sharing what I've learned. I love working with smokers. I love the craziness of tobacco addiction. This may seem politically incorrect: Current custom would enlist me in the tobacco wars, maybe as a general for the anti-smoking guys, but I refuse to serve in such a capacity. Rather, I see myself as a noncombatant who works with the refugees and refuses to bear arms.

As you'll read in this book, I recognize how tobacco initially—though perhaps not very efficiently—serves a good purpose, a higher purpose for our development. At parties, I often find myself outside by the rose bushes with the smokers, not because I want to smoke, and certainly not to try to drum up business, but rather just because I often find smokers to be more entertaining, more lively and fun.

Enlightenment?

In our culture, it is frowned upon to be enlightened. Or more precisely, to *talk* about being enlightened. Any book with the word *enlightened* in its title is bound to raise a few suspicions. After all, who can talk about enlightenment without sounding phony? In the *Tao Te Ching,* one of the oldest enlightenment books on the planet, Lao Tzu suggests, "He who knows, doesn't talk; he who talks, doesn't know." Since that time, saying anything about enlightenment has been tricky.

And similarly, in the Western tradition it's okay to say, "I am a Christian," but it's not okay to say, "I am Christlike," or "I let the mind in me be the same as that that was in Christ." We can't *say* it, but that's exactly what Christ commanded his followers to *do*! Doing it—living in the Christ-mind—is an enlightened way of living.

But it's not politically correct to say that, so let's talk instead about happiness. For our purposes, let's agree that the most enlightened person on Earth—the one who sees God, or the Buddha nature, or the universal harmony, or Christ in everything and everybody, all the time, everywhere, no matter what his or her own physical senses might report—surely must also be very happy. If enlightenment doesn't come with happiness, who needs it?

According to tradition, God doesn't change, but as we mature our perception of God changes. So just as there are degrees of enlightenment, of the perception of God, there are degrees of happiness. From a contemporary, street-mystic view, here's what it boils down to: If you are happy to be who you are, you are enlightened. If you are not happy to be who you are, you are endarkened. If you are happy to be who you are, all the time, every day, and even while you are dreaming, you are completely enlightened.

So what does this all have to do with smoking? For an enlightened view of that topic, turn the page!

1 Lighting Up for Enlightenment!
Introduction to the Seven-Step Journey

> Properly, we should read for power. Man reading should be
> man intensely alive.
> The book should be a ball of light in one's hand.
> —Ezra Pound

The basic premise of this book is that, regardless of your age at the time, you started smoking because you were looking for enlightenment. And surprise of surprises, you found it!

You found a new view of yourself, a wider view, a happier view, and even a truer view. Smoking *worked* to bring you into the next stage of life, the next stage of consciousness needed—demanded—by your own evolutionary impulses.

Do you remember how it was when you first started smoking? Even though your body rebelled and your social programming was setting off its own version of a car alarm, you were undoubtedly tickled to giggles with your new-found way of being in the world. It's no different for the yogi when he goes off to his cave: His body rebels, his social programming sets off its alarm, but he knows his quest for enlightenment is the best and most important thing he's ever done.

So the intent of this book is *not* to convince you to back off from the enlightenment you already have attained. You are not asked to stop being who you are or who you have been. Rather, what you'll find here will help you deepen and expand your natural enlightenment. You'll learn how to resume the adventure you started so many years ago. When you do that, your smoking will take care of itself: It will drop away on its own accord, at the right time, at the right place, almost effortlessly.

INSIGHT *Smoking becomes a problem for people only when their sense of adventure with it is interrupted.* (How long has it been since you viewed your smoking as an adventure?) *The smoking problem begins to dissolve as your sense of adventure resumes!*

One of my intentions in writing this book is to help you begin to reexperience that same excitement, newness, and expectancy with your smoking that you experienced when you first began experimenting with tobacco. And you can expect this new feeling of adventure to flow over into all other areas of your life. The adventure of creating, or discovering a "new" you begins again here, and the adventure will be as easy, as uncomplicated (and may feel just as "forbidden") as were your first experiments with tobacco. So, let's begin.

Your first assignment is this: Just relax!

Relax about whether or not you should smoke. As much as possible, just enjoy whatever your present smoking behavior may be and stop putting yourself down for doing it. Give yourself permission to simply enjoy these last days, or weeks, or months of companionship with your old friend, tobacco.

While that's a pretty easy assignment, it's also a radical one, isn't it? And here's the good news: The assignments and exercises in this book don't ever get any tougher than this! Guaranteed!

In *Magical Mind, Magical Body*, Deepak Chopra writes:

The first thing I would tell to someone trying to give up cigarettes is do not *try* to give up smoking. Hard-minded determination just sets you up for failure. . . . You have to retrain yourself as unconsciously as you started. . . . Keep your cigarettes with you.

By just relaxing and enjoying yourself, you're beginning the *easiest* stop-smoking process ever invented!

If you do the assignments and exercises suggested in this book, in the very near future you, too, may find yourself simply *forgetting* to smoke. As you magnify your own enlightenment—your naturally happy and adventurous self—you'll soon find it very easy, very ordinary, simply to walk away from your tobacco habit the same way you would walk away from a pile of leaves you had just finished raking, bagging, and putting out by the curb. When the job's done, you forget it, go on with your life—no big deal.

"Enlightenment is your ordinary mind," Zen Master Huang Po observed. Daibai asked Baso, "What is the Buddha?" Baso answered, "The mind is the Buddha."

In this book you'll discover how to dissolve your cigarette habit using your ordinary mind, your ordinary enlightenment or natural happiness. But even though you will rely on your ordinary, daily self, this *will* be a new adventure.

By reawakening your original impetus for smoking—your original quest for adventure, for enlightenment—you will quit with much less effort and agony than that to which the current dogma about cigarette addiction would condemn you. From classes I have taught, I have abundant proof that this reawakening process works! And works consistently.

Consciously tuning into your own happiness, your natural enlightenment, is like turning on a powerful, yet gentle, internal electric current that flows according to natural, obvious, unstoppable principles. For some smokers the enlightenment process works very quickly, in a matter of days or even hours. For other smokers it will unfold over a number of weeks or months. But the process does work for *every* smoker because it is based on the smoker's own daily natural behavior. You won't be relying on will power, outside motivation, or some strange strategy to find freedom from tobacco. Rather, you'll be using your own ordinary physical, emotional, and mental routines to discover the ancient secrets of freedom.

So whether this enlightenment process works quickly or over the long haul, it *will* work for you. So relax, have a smoke if you want, and let's get on with it.

The Spontaneous Seven-Step Program

Simply reading this book, you're going to learn everything you need to know about how to forget to smoke. Along the way, to make your learning more powerful, you'll be given the option of doing simple exercises and assignments that are designed to help you put into practice what you have just learned. You'll find yourself moving spontaneously through seven very easy steps:

1. Read the book.
2. Study the text.
3. Complete the exercises.
4. Share something of what you've learned with another smoker.
5. Begin regular journal-writing—*your* version of it.
6. Recognize, create, and re-create personal smoking rituals.

7. Day by day, hour by hour, experience yourself *forgetting to smoke*.

As you can see, there's nothing too tough about any of these steps. No wiggling your ears, no holding your breath for three days straight. You may not understand yet what we are talking about in the later steps, but Steps Six and Seven will be just as easy as Step One.

Step One: Read the book

If you've come this far, you're already doing Step One; just reading this book will prove to be enough for many smokers. These people will simply say, "Oh yes, I see now where I was hung up, so I'm not hung up there any more. Great! That's what I needed. Thank you. Goodbye."

Stopping smoking has been just that easy for many people, and it could be for you. While reading the book, you may find that a single sentence, a particular chapter, or the way something is said makes you think of something completely unrelated, but which nevertheless does the trick. Then—bingo—you're spontaneously free of whatever it was that kept you addicted to smoking, and you just set the cigarettes down and walk away. Why not? *There is no wrong way to find your natural freedom!*

But don't expect some outside force to come in and wrench your smokes away from you. When you stop smoking it will be *you* who stops, *you* who calls the shots, picks the time, the place, the reasons. But it won't be hard for you to do it; in fact, using an enlightened approach, you'll *enjoy* the process.

We have millions and millions of ex-smokers on the planet today. A study by the U.S. Center for Disease Control reported that 85 percent of them claim that they quit smoking on their own, without professional help or outside assistance. The truth is that *every* smoker who quits, does so on his or her own, so you will, too.

It's like being born and dying. While you can have people in attendance on both sides of the veil to guide you in the transition, help you, make you comfortable, and remove the blocks, the fundamental move is *yours*. You do it because the time and the place are right for you and because your life is ready for the next stage. No one can be born for you, just as no one can take on your death. That's part of the deal here. The same is true for stopping smoking.

Step Two: Study the text

The second step is just as effortless as the first. After reading the book for a while, you'll spontaneously start to think more deeply and actually *study* what has been written. You'll probably find yourself going back to reread the sections that intrigue you most, and then do the exercises you didn't do the first time through. You'll want to know: Was he really saying—and *meaning*—those radical things? Surely he didn't mean that I should actually enjoy my smoking? Where was that again? And why? Or, what did he mean when he wrote that starting smoking and stopping smoking were different ends of the same adventure? How could that apply to me, right now, right here?

Studying the text is different from simply reading the book. It entails consciously opening your mind and your heart to it, *wanting* to discover the truth about your smoking habit.

But you don't need to do that yet. You're still on Step One, so just read. Make it easy on yourself. Hang out with this book for awhile. Just relax. In the enlightenment tradition this is called *sat-*

sang, which is a Sanskrit word meaning "the company of truth." If you just hang out "in the company of truth," your mind and body spontaneously begin to reverberate. As a beginner, you aren't expected to do anything but be here.

It's like showing up for church, or going to the feet of the master, or reading scripture. In *satsang*, you find yourself inspired to do what is most natural for you. So relax. Hang out.

How to Relax about Your Smoking

`INSIGHT` *There's only one way to relax about anything, including smoking: Think thoughts you enjoy thinking. Take a vacation from the thoughts you don't enjoy!*

If you're lying on a white beach in the Bahamas, under green palm trees next to a blue lagoon, but you're thinking thoughts you don't enjoy and that make you uptight, you're not relaxing. On the other hand, if you're in a downtown rush-hour traffic jam, horns honking, brakes squealing, but you're thinking about your lover's lovely words last night, you're relaxing.

If you're a smoker in any developing country in the world, you are bombarded daily with thoughts you don't enjoy about smoking. They may be spoken or unspoken. They may originate with you, or they might come from your family, your neighbor, or some government agency a thousand miles away. Regardless of where they come from, if you're not enjoying your thoughts about smoking, you're not relaxing! And if you're not relaxing, enjoying your happiness, you're not practicing enlightenment, nor are you forgetting to smoke.

Paradoxical as it might sound, rehearsing thoughts about how *bad* smoking is for you is one way to keep yourself trapped! A Gallup poll sponsored by *American Health* magazine and the Campbell's Soup Company found that, "More people change their habits because they feel good about themselves and want to feel still better than because they fear the health (or social) consequences of their current lifestyle."

If you're like most smokers, you've been condemning yourself about your smoking, consciously or subconsciously, for years. This is *not* an enlightened approach to your life or to your smoking habit, for the simple reason that it doesn't work. In fact, your basic tobacco habit is a *habit of thoughts.* It has become a habitual, generally unenjoyable way of thinking about yourself, and more particularly about your smoking. Such a way of thinking drains your energy, narrows your perspective, and dims your lights. You generally think such thoughts because you assume you are *supposed* to be thinking them. You have been educated to think these thoughts that you don't enjoy about smoking. You've been taught to believe that if you don't continue to think them, you'll be putting yourself in danger.

The truth is that you are putting yourself in the greatest danger of physical disease and emotional and mental imbalance when you habitually think thoughts you don't enjoy, whether about smoking or anything else. Even if these thoughts are so-called true thoughts, or are based on supposed fact, holding on to what you do not enjoy does neither you nor anybody else any good!

Here's the test: Have the tens of thousands of thoughts you've had year after year about how bad smoking is for you successfully led you to quit? The answer must be No, or you wouldn't be reading this book.

Sure, you may have badgered yourself into quitting once or twice, even three or four times, forcing yourself to quit by thinking thoughts about how bad smoking is for you. But that is the least powerful, least effective way to quit, and often it is so unsatisfactory that you eventually return to smoking.

Currently, the primary strategy of almost every other stop-smoking program is to first frighten the smoker into deciding to quit. This is the reason why there is such a low success rate in most of these programs! In fact, a survey by the U.S. Center for Disease Control found that the average success rate for all programs, including the patch, hypnosis, and acupuncture, was only 8 percent!

So what we are doing in this first chapter is giving you reasons—the emotional encouragement and intellectual underpinnings—why you should think thoughts you enjoy about your smoking. Take a vacation from the thoughts you don't enjoy about your smoking.

It's an unusual, even radical approach. But obviously, you need a radically different approach. Since it is different from anything you've been taught is "right," you'll have to be courageous to try it. You'll have to be just as brave as you were when, years ago, contrary to what you'd been taught, you agreed to try your first cigarette.

But from my perspective, trying to talk you into this approach is like trying to talk you into eating strawberry shortcake with whipped cream! I don't see why there should be any argument!

But again, you're still working on Step One—reading the book. Don't relax if you don't want to. Don't take a vacation. Think what you like. Stay as uptight as you want. You're the boss.

If your habit of beating yourself up about your smoking is so ingrained that you just can't stop it, then what you can do is start enjoying beating yourself up!

As you'll discover throughout this book, joy is the key to enlightenment, to freedom, and to stopping smoking. So if you insist on beating yourself up, at least enjoy yourself while you're doing it! This is our Zenlike strategy.

When you start studying this material, rather than just reading it, you'll probably do so quite spontaneously, without conscious decision, without having to force yourself. You'll start studying this book simply because you naturally enjoy studying it. We rely on your spontaneous joy for every step of this program.

Step Three: Complete the exercises

When I suggest that you relax, think about what you enjoy about smoking, and take a vacation from all those thoughts you don't enjoy, how hard is that? You either feel like doing it or you don't. All exercises in this book are designed that way: They are meant to be fun, natural, obvious approaches to your smoking that you will be excited to try, to experiment with, maybe rearrange or redesign to suit your own style and personality, but close enough to your own smoking life that they ring a bell.

This whole enlightenment journey is designed to help you do what you most love to do, what's easy for you to do, natural for you, without requiring a lot of effort or will power. At each stage of the journey, you are given very tiny baby steps that will allow you simply to walk away from the tobacco struggle.

The program you'll find in this book is so simple and easy that you don't even need to go through all seven steps if you don't want. You can go directly from Step One to Step Seven just because it happens to suit your mood to give the whole thing up today! Or you can go from Step One to Step Two and then to Step Seven. In fact, you can go to Step Seven at any time you choose during the enlightenment process.

It's also perfectly permissible to go through all six steps and then decide that you're still not ready to forget to smoke, that you'd enjoy taking a little more time with this whole process. You may choose to start over from the beginning or to go back to any of the preceding steps that you particularly enjoyed and do them over again. In this process, we assume that you, as an enlightened being, are at least somewhat in control of your life and that whatever you decide is best for you is in fact best for you.

This book is designed to free you of smoking in the first reading, but you are free to take as long as you want with it. You may choose to do it in eight hours, eight days, or eight months. This is a life-changing process! Let it take as long as it takes and just enjoy it, quick or long!

Step Four: Share something of what you've learned with another smoker

There's and old saying, "If you want to learn something, teach it." Sharing something of this book with other smokers should be a fun, spontaneous, "no-brainer" event. Sure, as the author of this book you'd expect me to suggest that you buy ten more copies and pass them out to your smoker friends. But there's also a metaphysical (*enlightened*) principle at work here: *What blesses one, blesses all.* In other words, a blessing for one person won't ever result in deprivation for somebody else. You'll discover that sharing your experience, not necessarily by giving away a book, but with just a word or a laugh, is helpful not only to those smokers you share it with, but even more so for your own understanding of what we're doing here.

When you outwardly share information with others, it helps clarify and internalize it for you. By sharing what you're learning, putting it in your own words, using your own analogies and stories, you'll discover that the principles have become more and more operative in your life.

Alcoholics Anonymous (AA) has a long history proving the efficacy of one addicted person helping another. They encourage "reaching out" by sharing stories fairly early in the twelve-step program, because their experience has shown that talking to others, helping others, internalizes and empowers the process.

Over the centuries, those on the path of enlightenment have recognized three fundamental components that are necessary (or at least very, very helpful) for the success of their journey:

1. A teacher
2. A teaching
3. The community which arises around the teacher and the teaching.

None of these is absolutely essential for enlightenment, for freedom, but they have proven to be very helpful and effective for countless seekers over many centuries.

In this process you are encouraged to let your own inner happiness be your teacher, your guru. Learning from your own happiness, you learn at your own pace, in your own words, exactly what is most helpful to you at this time. During this season in your life, this particular book functions as the basic teaching. Your teacher, which is your own happiness, will show you the best way to apply this particular teaching in your daily life. Both teacher and teaching will become a lot more fun, efficient, and effective when you share the adventure with a friend or two or three.

But don't worry. As you work with the principles in this book, natural forces are set in motion that will probably bring you into contact with one or more other smokers who are just as ready as you are for this radically happy approach. You may find yourself making the first move in bringing up the subject, but don't be surprised if other smokers bring it up first. Take this as a sign that it's okay to share what you're learning here. Don't hesitate to tell them about your doubts as well as your hopes for this enlightened approach.

Put a group together if you want. Study the book. Meet regularly. Make it fun! You'll discover that the enlightenment teaching is much more casual, upbeat, and laissez-faire than AA, which, as we all know, has saved hundreds of thousands of lives. But our approach is quite different.

As you've already glimpsed, the enlightenment program does not try to pressure you into quitting. As a matter of fact, one of our basic strategies is to *relieve the pressure* you may feel about your smoking.

Here's why: The pressure to quit (both internally and externally) is one of the primary reasons it's so hard to quit! It's a basic law of nature—Newton's Third Law of Thermodynamics: For every action, there's an equal and opposite reaction! In other words: Pressure to Quit = Pressure to Continue!

The person who puts the most pressure on you about your smoking is always you yourself.

If you're like most smokers, you beat yourself up, put yourself down, and twist yourself inside out about your smoking, at least a little, every day. And it doesn't do any good!

This book will teach you how and why to consciously *stop doing that*, and thus be free of the smoking struggle. So part of your sharing with other smokers will be a sharing of good news, of the peace treaty you've signed with yourself in regard to the tobacco wars!

Step Five: Begin regular journal-writing—*your* version of it

In the beginning was the Word, and the Word was with God, and the Word was God.
—John 1.1

Beginning in the Middle Ages, up until relatively recently, the primary motivation for teaching people to read was to enable them to read the scriptures on their own. In the same way, a fundamental reason for learning to write is so that you might write scriptures on your own—to write inspired, life-transforming words that waken you to reality.

The fifth step, in which you begin doing regular journal-keeping or its equivalent, is again a process that you will probably find yourself *wanting* to experiment with. It won't be a matter of mustering up self-discipline or agreeing to self-sacrifice but rather it will be a welcome adventure, with new sights and tastes and smells, that makes you feel more alive than you have felt in decades!

Is keeping a journal absolutely necessary or mandatory? No. But if you'd been wandering around in the city for years, and knew that if you could only find the road out you'd immediately return to your country home, wouldn't you be grateful for a map of the territory? That's what we're offering—a map of the territory—and a journal helps you find out where you are on that map.

Step Six: Recognize, create, and re-create your personal smoking rituals

Step Six will also help you pinpoint where you are on the map in relation to the exit. The practice of recognizing and honoring your personal smoking rituals is based on the principle that: *you cannot master what you do not love!* In this step you'll learn how to make your smoking a lot more enjoyable as well as a lot less debilitating, both physically and emotionally. This is the step—the process— that allows you to approach this whole process, and the dissolution of your own smoking patterns, very carefully, slowly, tenderly, at just the pace to make it work!

Before the monk is allowed into the monastery, or the nun into the nunnery, he or she has already started practicing in his or her own daily life the reverence and prayerfulness that will be intensified in the more structured setting. Being prayerful and reverent about your smoking patterns—i.e., not beating yourself up about your current lifestyle—is the first step out of such patterns.

If, during the first reading of this book, you don't yet feel ready to actually quit, Step Six will render your smoking a lot less distressing, both physically and mentally, both for yourself and for those around you. Practicing Step Six, you'll find yourself *enjoying* your smoking more and, consequently, *doing* it less!

It is more likely, however, that in the process of reading this book you will discover the hidden keys that open the locks of your smoking habit in such a way that you'll find yourself free of tobacco addiction. Especially if you've been wanting to quit before reading this book, or at least you've been wanting *to want to quit.* You'll discover that this book lays out the easiest, most commonsense and effective way ever developed to dissolve the smoking habit. Chances are, by reading this book you will recognize how easy it can be, and find yourself just doing it!

An Overview

Undoubtedly, by now you've recognized that this approach to quitting smoking is completely different from anything you've encountered before. Here's an overview of the revolutionary stop-smoking philosophy you are about to experience:

- No scare tactics
- No unhappy health warnings
- No will power–based strategies
- No forcing yourself to do something you are not happy to do
- The enlightened path is both effortless and the most efficient path
- Spontaneous healing, as well as more gradual, unfolding healings will manifest themselves
- Simple awareness exercises will lead you to healing and forgetting to smoke.

Step Seven: Day by day, hour by hour, experience yourself forgetting to smoke

Experiencing yourself forgetting to smoke is a *conscious* and *deliberate* process you will learn to do and want to do as a result of the accumulated insights and exercises you encounter throughout the book. You learn to forget to smoke in the same way you learned to walk—not all at once, but one step at a time; one step after another. When you were first learning to walk, it was a strange and awkward and somewhat off-balancing affair. Once you actually learned, however, it was the most natural thing in the world. The same holds true for learning to forget to smoke!

Because you are an adult, motivated and ready, you can learn this process very quickly. Nevertheless, your current stage in learning to forget to smoke might be viewed as the infant stage, where before you walk you still need to learn to sit up, roll over, crawl, stand up, move out. You will learn to forgive yourself for smoking in the past, enjoy your smoking now, and look forward to a smokeless future without anxiety. But these are in fact new positions you'll be learning—new attitudes, new ways of "balancing" your inner world in regard to smoking. So there is no need to rush yourself.

Don't worry about the timing. You *will* experience yourself forgetting to smoke. When you look back on it, it will seem as if it all happened quite effortlessly, on your own. Just as now you get up and walk to the refrigerator quite naturally and gracefully.

So if in the journey you are about to take you discover one day that you have fallen, that doesn't mean you aren't still learning to walk! After you've fallen crawl around for a while, if that's what moves you. Or find something to help prop yourself up. Learning to forget to smoke, like learning to walk, is a season you go through that, once you're on the other side, gives you an immense amount of freedom…just like enlightenment!

Here's some more good news: As a smoker (soon to be ex-smoker), the freedom you're about to experience will be much deeper, finer, and more delicious than anything you might have experienced if you had never been a smoker! In this journey you will learn to honor your past years of *smoking* as well as to enjoy future years of *not* smoking. There was something you needed, wanted, and *received* from smoking that kept you at it. There's no sense—no joy—in putting yourself down because of it. You do it. You smoke. You like it. So be it. Now you're going to forget it. Life changes.

====

Exercises

Lighten Up Your Lighting Up!

As mentioned earlier, your first assignment is to enjoy your thoughts about smoking and to take a vacation from those thoughts concerning smoking that you don't enjoy. If you're like most smokers, you've been replaying thoughts you don't enjoy way too long and it's time to take a breather.

So at least for the time it takes to read this book, whenever you find yourself thinking something you don't enjoy about your smoking, just drop it! Forget it! Don't try to figure it out, justify it, or rationalize it. Just drop it! Take a vacation. Move on to thinking about something more enjoyable. That's the first—and the last, and the most powerful—suggestion. The first work is to relax, to enjoy yourself more than you have been.

The following exercises are designed to help you lighten up a bit about your smoking. For most smokers, it's hard just to forget about smoking all at once. So you need to start changing your relationship with it gradually. And you want to change it for the better.

Tobacco is like a spouse you're about ready to divorce. At the end, it's time to lighten up and not take the relationship so seriously. Get out of the old ruts, bring back the love. Have some fun for a change.

Upon first reading these exercises, you might think, That's silly, I can't do that. But suppose you had never seen anybody smoke... ever, and a friend came up with a cigarette, and said, let's put some flame on the end of this and suck it into our lungs. How silly would *that* sound? So when we talk *silly*, or *childish*, let's put it into some perspective.

While you aren't required to do these exercises yet, if you should find yourself spontaneously doing some of them during the next few days, don't hold back. Give yourself to them. Why not? You have nothing to lose but your chain (smoking).

Ten Somewhat Goofy Lightening Up Exercises

The point of these exercises is to loosen you up; expand and enliven your mental, emotional, and physical smoking routines; let you have *fun* again with your smoking! (Here at the start of the teaching, most smokers are still too uptight and rigid with their habits to give themselves the freedom to do all ten exercises right away. If that's your case, just do the ones that look like fun!)

1. Pretend your *next* cigarette is your *first* cigarette. Give it that much attention, that much joy. Pretend you are a kid again with your first smoke. Grin, feel naughty and excited about it.

2. Pretend you are standing in front of a firing squad and your *next* cigarette is going to be your *last* cigarette. Your good times on Earth are just about over. The angels are hovering nearby. Inhale deeply, richly, satisfied with your time in the flesh. Enjoy this last moment of your life, and your last cigarette.

3. Alternate throughout the day: *This is my first cigarette ever.... This is my last cigarette ever.*

4. With your first cigarette in the morning say, "Hello, old friend. I love you." To your last cigarette at night say, "Goodnight, old friend. I love you."

5. Pretend you are a ventriloquist. When you say "I love you," to your cigarettes, morning and night, have them respond, "I love you, too," right back.

6. If you're still smoking indoors, buy a new, fancy ashtray for your favorite smoking chair, and one for every other corner of your house. Or get a new one for your porch, or car, or wherever you most regularly smoke. Tell yourself, I love smoking! I deserve a new ashtray!

7. Keep your new ashtrays clean, with books of matches or lighters nearby, as if you were momentarily expecting a visit from an important guest who smokes.

8. Next time you buy a pack of smokes, tell the cashier, "I'm happy to spend my money on these babies. I love them. I

really do." Don't back down, just grin, and stick with your confession.

9. Pretend that you quit five years ago and that now you have no desire whatsoever to smoke, but someone is putting a gun to your head and making you do it. To save your life, smoke a cigarette.

10. Pretend you are a monkey who has been taught to smoke. Make big lips as you exhale. Then pretend you are a movie star who smokes. Be really cool and sophisticated. Alternate between the smoking monkey and the smoking movie star.

As you'll learn in the next lesson, enjoying yourself more *while* smoking is the first step in enjoying yourself *not* smoking! What have you got to lose? For that, read on.

2 How to Forget to Smoke
The Basic Enlightenment Exercise

> These things have I spoken unto you, that my joy might remain
> in you, and that your joy might be full.
> —John 15.11

What you have to lose by studying this material is the unhappiness—both yours and everybody else's—that currently surrounds smoking. When this unhappiness falls away, you will experience the freedom either to smoke or not to smoke. When you enjoy yourself, you become the master—not the slave—in the tobacco game.

From long experience teaching smokers and having been a smoker myself for over twenty years, I know there are some readers who are ready right now, right here, to quit. Some readers want to skip Steps One through Six and go directly to Step Seven. No philosophy, no theory, no whys and wherefores. They just want to know, okay, how do I do it exactly? How do I quit? How do I "*forget to smoke*," for pity's sake? How do I take Step Seven? Other smokers, of course, aren't quite so eager.

Whether you're ready to quit right now, or whether you want to proceed at a more leisurely pace, it makes sense to learn what Step Seven entails. After all, what is the destination of this journey? Where are we heading?

Forgetting to Smoke

You already know how to forget to smoke. I'm sure you've done it hundreds of times, when you were at the movies, or playing a game, or rafting down a river. You forget to smoke when you are so happily involved with someone or something else that the idea of smoking doesn't even come up. If you could move into a state of "pleasurable forgetfulness" on purpose, wouldn't that be sweet?

The strategy outlined in this book helps you do exactly that. You can teach yourself to enjoy *not* smoking more than you enjoy smoking, but it's not an either/or situation. To enjoy not smoking more than you enjoy smoking, you have to practice enjoying everything in your life—including smoking—more intensely than you do now.

"Happiness is the goal of all goals," writes Deepak Chopra. "Addiction is nothing other than the linkage of certain stimulus with an interpretation of happiness or pleasure. How do you change it? By substituting the experience of pleasure with a stronger experience of pleasure!"

You already know that when you enjoy something intensely— a lover, or a movie, or a delicious dessert—that in that moment you forget about smoking. What we have discovered is that it is possible to enjoy yourself much more than you may have been taught (or allowed) by your family, your school, or your social culture.

At the Smoker's Freedom School, we have proven that you can consciously, deliberately *forget to smoke* when you increase your enjoyment of whatever else you are doing. You don't need will power or "force" to accomplish this, any more than you used will power or force to start smoking. Sure, there may have been some discomfort, but your first cigarette was something you *enjoyed* picking up. And you can experience the same sense of exhilaration as you learn to *enjoy* putting it down.

The Enlightenment Exercise*

As already mentioned, forgetting to smoke, or its equivalent, can be the spontaneous result of a deliberate, conscious exercise. You might enjoy thinking of it as a game you play with your inner thoughts, a game that sooner or later has the remarkable effect of freeing you from tobacco. In this book, we'll refer to this process as the "Enlightenment Exercise," or alternatively, the "Enlightenment Game," because that's exactly what it does: It magnifies your natural enlightenment, your natural happiness. What we've discovered is that as you magnify your enlightenment, or your natural happiness, your smoking habit loses power and, with even the most gentle nudge, falls away naturally, spontaneously, at exactly the right time, in the right way, at the right place. The smoking habit may drop off all at once, or it might fall away in bits and pieces. We have

---

* As I mentioned in the Introduction, I first learned the particular form of this exercise some years ago from Dr. Christian Almayrac, a delightfully, radically happy French physician who has demonstrated the beautiful power of this process for more than fifteen years, in his own life, in his family life, and with his students and patients on two continents. Many healings of a variety of ailments and many resolutions of social circumstances have been effected simply by the employment of this exercise. At The Smoker's Freedom School, it has been our pleasure to focus, test, and extend Dr. Almayrac's work for the specific benefit of smokers.

seen this process work time and time again for every type of smoker, and it will work for you!

The Enlightenment Exercise is composed of four parts or laws: The Law of Happiness, the Law of Linkage, the Law of Spontaneity, and the Law of Joyous Action.

The Law of Happiness

The Law of Happiness, which we encourage every student to memorize using the first person, states: *Enjoying my happiness is the most important thing for me and for everybody around me.* When applied to smoking, it means that *enjoying* your smoking is the most important thing you can do—contrary to what health officials might say. Indeed, enjoying your smoking is the first step in enjoying *not* smoking!

The Law of Happiness assumes that you are already happy and that you can consciously choose to enjoy your happiness. More broadly, the exercise assumes that you are already enlightened—already imbued with a divinely radiant, unlimited, joyful consciousness that you can access at will. Whether you agree or disagree with this assumption doesn't matter when it comes to the practical application of the exercise: It works for anybody who *uses it*, regardless of assumptions or mindset.

The Law of Linkage

> For as he thinketh in his heart, so is he.
> —Proverbs 23:7

This second part of the Enlightenment Exercise states: *I enjoy my happiness when I enjoy the thought I am thinking this moment*. Thus the Law of Linkage *links* your happiness with the thoughts you are thinking.

The Enlightenment Exercise reflects the fact that a divinely happy, divinely empowered consciousness is ours—yours—by grace. It's an aspect of your spirit, your soul. You don't have to work at it. Happiness was implanted in you long before your birth and will remain with you long after you have dropped your body, and even long after the sun has gone out. This happiness, this enlightenment is a quality of your eternal individuality. Whether an atheist, agnostic, or transcendental mystic, you enjoy your happiness when you enjoy the thoughts you are thinking. Conversely, you don't enjoy your happiness or yourself when you don't enjoy your thoughts.

You are *always* free and able to choose to enjoy your thoughts because enlightenment—or divine bliss, what the Hindus call *satchitananda* is the underlying nature of consciousness itself. For various reasons—our training, our culture, our karma—we often forget this underlying aspect of our consciousness, or ignore it or deny it outright. Yet, forgetfulness or denial or ignorance of enlightenment does not change the fact that you are already natively enlightened, blissful.

Assumptions of our inherent bliss have been shared by the best of the sages and seers, wise men and masters, from every culture and from nearly every spiritual tradition throughout history. For example, many Christians call this joyful consciousness the "Christ within." Hindus call it the *atman*. Buddhists call it *satori*, or the Buddha mind. Jews call it "Immanuel," the Presence of God. Don Juan Matus called it *"seeing."* Krishnamurti called it "Being." This consciousness—this joy—is the life spark, the natural happiness that each of us has, that each of us fundamentally is: pure, transcendental, beautiful.

Paramahansa Yogananda, one of the first to bridge the spiritual traditions of East and West, in his classic text, *Autobiography of a Yogi*, writes, "Because the very nature of God is Bliss, the man in attunement with Him experiences a native, boundless Joy."

From my own experiences and from the experiences of friends, students, and fellow travelers on this path to magnified experience of happiness, I know that when we give priority to this enlightened aspect of consciousness, to this joyous life spark, and then work to fan the spark into flame, great wisdom and freedom enter all areas of our lives, and specifically in this context, enhanced enlightenment brings wisdom and then freedom from tobacco addiction.

The Law of Spontaneity

If enjoying your happiness is the most important thing for you and for those around you, and if you enjoy your happiness or enlightenment only when you enjoy the thoughts you are thinking in each moment, then one of the most important questions in your life, if not *the* most important question is, Am I enjoying my thought, yes or no? The third part of the Enlightenment Exercise states: *Whenever necessary, I ask myself, am I enjoying this thought, yes or no? If the answer is not an immediate and spontaneous "yes," then it's a "no."*

Dr. Almayrac explains that since happiness is the most important thing in your life, you need to have a clear, high, and unmistakable test or standard by which to ensure that you are presently enjoying happiness. For something so important, you don't ever want there to be any doubt. That's why the answer must be an immediate and spontaneous "yes," or it's a "no."

Binary Processing

As we all know, computers have the enviable ability to process all types of information at very high speeds with almost perfect accuracy. Computers work on a simple principle called "binary processing." Computer codes or "languages" are based on the binary system, with the only "words" being 0 and 1. When running a program, the computer responds based on the order of the "words." And when processing information, the computer selects between only two choices—two "bits" of information—at one time. Every computer works this way, from the handheld calculator to the mammoth pieces of equipment that sent astronauts to the Moon.

Binary processing is perhaps the most efficient way to process information. In fact, binary processing may be the most efficient way for us to think and to create. Unlike computers, we humans process not only what we have learned (i.e., "inputted" information), but we also create new thoughts, new forms of information and inspiration, new worlds altogether. In this respect, our processes or thoughts are more complex and our choices more difficult than those of a computer.

In developing and refining the Enlightenment Exercise, Dr. Almayrac created a "binary processing tool" to simplify all this, a tool that allows us to access our innate happiness, our natural enlightenment immediately, easily, continually, and with ever-increasing efficiency. It is the Law of Spontaneity: *Whenever necessary, I ask myself, am I enjoying this thought, yes or no? If the answer is not an immediate and spontaneous "yes," then it's a "no."*

Generally, when you are enjoying yourself—be it with your lover, your friends, sports, hobbies, whatever—the question of whether you are enjoying yourself does not come up. So if the answer to the question is spontaneously, Yes, I'm enjoying myself, I'm enjoying my thought, simply continue doing whatever you're doing, thinking whatever you're thinking. Life is good. This is how it's supposed to be!

The question is most useful, however, when you find yourself uncomfortable, or just bored, or nervous, or uptight, *not* enjoying yourself, not enjoying your thoughts for one reason or another (as, for instance, when you have just given up smoking!). By asking the question—*am I enjoying this thought, yes or no?* you become more self-aware, you immediately recognize what you are doing, what you are thinking at this particular moment. And this recognition leads you to the next binary processing mechanism of the Enlightenment Exercise: the Law of Joyous Action.

The Law of Joyous Action

The fourth and final part of the Enlightenment Exercise states: *If I discover I am not enjoying my thought, I have two options: (1.) I can choose to drop the thought that I do not enjoy, and choose instead a thought that I enjoy more; or (2.) I can choose to enjoy the thought that I was not enjoying a moment before.*

As we'll explore in later chapters, smoking addiction is first and foremost a habitual way of thinking and only secondarily a physiological or cellular dependence. It's as if you have three jagged, notched gears—mental, emotional, and physical—turning on each other, a well-oiled machine that keeps your addiction active.

Physically giving up smoking before your mental and emotional patterns are dismantled inevitably results in a screeching and grinding halt in your physical body. Even though the physical gear isn't turning—even though you aren't physically smoking—your mental and emotional gears still struggle to churn, now clanging and banging because the third gear is no longer doing its part.

If, before you physically give up smoking, your mental and emotional "smoking gears" are smoothed and polished—which happens as you consciously choose thoughts you enjoy and consciously release thoughts you don't enjoy—you'll discover that the physiological and cellular reactions of your physical body are easily accommodated, and even blissful, when you give up smoking.

The Philosophy

The principle behind the Enlightenment Exercise, as I'm sure you've noticed, is not new. It may be presented here in a different, simplified, nonsectarian form, or perhaps in a different verbal style than what you have heard before. As Dr. Almayrac has said in numerous lectures, "What I say out loud you already know in your heart." Because the Enlightenment Exercise is based on universal principles, you may already be doing something very similar to it in your daily life.

In the Zen tradition, it is recognized that an authentic, bona fide enlightened person occasionally appears, seemingly out of nowhere, without training, without lineage, without credentials, simply because enlightenment is inherent within each of us, ready to be realized, actualized. In the Zen tradition, the enlightenment of such beings (or more precisely, the *realization* of their enlightenment) is honored, accepted, cherished, and seen as no less valid than that which has been brought about through the "traditional disciplines" of recognized teachers and monasteries.

Nevertheless, most "realization," or actualization of enlightenment, even in the Zen tradition, comes about when one person comes into contact with the flame of enlightenment that burns in another. With such contact, the "kindling" that has been prepared in the student is lit. With the help of a teacher and a teaching, the student, too, becomes self-radiant, and the need for outside fire no longer exists (though such added light adds beauty and depth.)

The same is true with smoking. Once we learned how to use tobacco, we did not need to be further taught, or encouraged, or led, again and again.

Once the proper "use" of tobacco was shown to us, didn't we use it even when we were alone? We might have been far from civilization, or with others who themselves did not smoke, but still, we smoked. We took our "light" and our smoke with us wherever we went.

So, too, with the Enlightenment Exercise. Once we have taken it up, we can experience its pleasure no matter where we are, who we are with, or what we are doing. And when we share our happiness with others, it adds depth, beauty, and camaraderie to our relationships and to whatever we are doing. So, are we suggesting that this exercise is something that can replace tobacco? Absolutely, Yes!

The Process

When you begin practicing the Enlightenment Exercise, you will discover first that it makes your tobacco use more enjoyable, and then that it makes *everything* more enjoyable. With additional practice, you will find that the pleasure you receive from this exercise is more powerful and more immediate than the pleasure you receive from smoking. And even better, that if and when you choose, you can use this new pleasure to eliminate your smoking habit entirely!

After all, your thoughts about tobacco are what make stopping tobacco use most difficult, most uncomfortable. So again, How do you do it? How do you quit smoking? How do you *forget to smoke?* It's simple!

- Train yourself to enjoy your thoughts, one at a time and then in clusters. You can accomplish this training quickly or over a period of weeks or months.

- Teach yourself to enjoy what comes to mind when you think about a quit date. Train yourself to view your quit date, not with fear and loathing, as has probably been your habit, but rather with simple, happy expectation.

- Teach yourself to enjoy what happens to you, inside and out, after you lay the tobacco down.

- Teach yourself to enjoy everything about the whole process, and because your joy is the essence of enlightenment itself, you'll discover that you don't need to struggle or fight or battle with yourself over this issue. Just do it, one thought, one step at a time.

- Enjoy yourself, and by doing so consciously, deliberately forget to smoke.

At The Smoker's Freedom School, smoker after smoker has found freedom from tobacco in just this way. You are free to use the nicotine patch, or the inhaler, or the gum, or any other aid that your happiness leads you to employ. You can also ask others to join you in the quitting game. We've found, however, that nothing extra is necessary—no patch, no companion, no special diet—only sincere joy in the process.

If you are so inclined, you can take Step Seven right now, right here, without knowing anything more than you already know. And you'd probably find it easy. There's no law that says you can't be happy to quit right here at the start of the book. You can enjoy and be successful at quitting right now because happiness, joy, is your native consciousness; it has been with you forever. So, using your joy, quitting right now doesn't need to be a big deal. You are free just to do it. Think what you enjoy, quit smoking, and get on with your life!

On the other hand, you're probably still on Step One—happy just reading the book, hanging out, seeing what there is to see. That, too, is perfectly expressed happiness.

The Basic Exercise

We always recommend to students that they memorize the Enlightenment Exercise at the outset. Just by reading this book you'll probably have it pretty well memorized by the time you reach the last page. But if you take time out now to memorize it, you'll discover that during your daily life simple recollection of the form of the exercise will spontaneously lead you to *perform* the exercise. You'll discover that just repeating these particular words leads you into a freer, happier frame of mind. And that frame of mind, as should be clear by now, is the motivating force on this path to liberation.

The Enlightenment Exercise

1. The Law of Happiness. *Enjoying my happiness is the most important thing for me and for everybody around me.*

2. The Law of Linkage. *I enjoy my happiness when I enjoy the thought I am thinking in this moment.*

3. The Law of Spontaneity. *Whenever necessary, I ask myself, Am I enjoying this thought, yes or no? If the answer is not an immediate and spontaneous "yes," then it's a "no."*

4. The Law of Joyous Action. *If I discover I am not enjoying my thought right now, then I am not free.*
   a. *I can choose to drop the thought that I do not enjoy, and choose instead a thought that I enjoy more;* or
   b. *I can choose to enjoy the thought that I was not enjoying a moment before, either as it is, or by changing its form, size, texture, position, place, or voice.*

You will notice that we have added a few new ways for you to enjoy a thought that you didn't enjoy before. Try them!

Richard Bandler, in his classic little book *Using Your Brain—For a Change*, writes:

Most people don't actively and deliberately use their own brains. Your brain is like a machine without an "off switch." If you don't give it something to do, it just runs on and on.... Most people are prisoners of their own brains. It's as if they are chained to the last seat of the bus and someone else is driving.

Bandler suggests fourteen different ways to change the visual appearance of a thought. Consider these suggestions as they relate to the way you think about smoking.

1. *Color*. You can "color" a thought with one particular color or a bunch of different colors. You can make it brightly colored, or put it into black and white.

2. *Distance*. Make the thought up close or far away.

3. *Depth*. Make a thought intensely three-dimensional, or make it into a line drawing.

4. *Duration*. Make a quick thought last longer; make a lasting thought disappear quickly.

5. *Clarity*. Change from crystal clear to fuzzy, or vice versa.

6. *Contrast*. Blend the thought into itself, or make the parts distinct; change the contrasts.

7. *Scope*. Put the thought in a tiny little frame, or see it in three dimensions all around your head, or view it from (or in) outer space.

8. *Movement*. Change it from a still photo to a movie, or vice versa.

9. *Speed*. Adjust the speed of the movie—fast or slow.

10. *Hue*. Change the color patterns, emphasize the reds, or the greens, or the blues, or the bright whites, dim grays.

11. *Transparency*. Make your thoughts see-through, or like lead.

12. *Aspect ratio*. Make a framed picture tall and narrow, then short and wide.

13. *Orientation*. Tilt the top of the thought away from you, and then toward you.

14. *Foreground/background*. Give your thoughts new pictures

to play in—give them happy foregrounds, or backgrounds, or both.

When you begin playing with your thoughts about smoking in this way, using your joy as the "navigator," as the game master, you will discover that thoughts you have never been able to enjoy before are now amusing, quite easily played with, and thus no longer burdensome.

The Enlightenment Game, or exercise, may seem a little too corny, a little too easy, a little too "airy" for you at this point. Or, it may seem the exact right path, the one you've been looking for. Or, it may seem far too difficult.

However this approach feels to you right now, all you have to do is just hang out, see what happens. No matter what you're feeling, if you keep reading, you will pick up insights that will absolutely move you down the path to freedom.

In the next chapter, you'll be introduced to an easy process that helps bring the Enlightenment Exercise down to Earth, making it even more powerful for the work at hand. After that, you'll learn why nicotine (despite all the publicity and lawsuits) is not the real culprit behind smoking, and why nicotine patches, inhalers, and gum work for some people but not for others.

Keep reading... and have fun. We've only just begun!

3 In the Beginning Was the Word . . .

> Words are the most powerful drug used by mankind.
> —Rudyard Kipling

Let's begin this chapter with a few simple exercises.

First, I encourage you to purchase, or recycle, a notebook or journal or even a pad of paper that you will dedicate to your new smoking adventure. Your freedom from smoking is a topic worthy of study, just as you would for a college course. Would you attempt to take—or more precisely, pass—a college course without taking notes? Of course not! So get a journal and dust off your favorite pen! At the very least, you can use the journal to keep a diary about this long-awaited season of smoking cessation. Are you ready?

Okay, now that you have something to write on, list your ten most-unwanted thoughts about smoking. Write down the ten things you do not enjoy, things that bother you, that make you feel unhappy or irritated about your smoking. Ideally, these ten thoughts are not strangers to you but, rather, are your unwelcome *daily* companions, your dark daily musings about your smoking. It is best if you can capture on paper—word for word—the actual thoughts about smoking that replay themselves over and over and over again in your daily life. To accomplish this, you may need a day or two to become mindful of your thoughts, to hear your inner voice, to recognize the form your ten most unwanted thoughts generally assume.

Sure, that's asking you to do a lot of work, here in Chapter 3, when we hardly know each other. If you're still on Step One—just reading, hanging out—you probably won't do these two little exercises yet. But maybe this is your second reading, or you are already convinced that you want to move into this Enlightenment process a little deeper, right away, here, now, because you're anxious to be free. If you've written out your ten most-unwanted thoughts and three wanted thoughts for each of those, good! Welcome to the fun house!

When you are spontaneously moved by your own joy to do this exercise, you discover that the ten most-unwanted thoughts about your smoking are slippery little guys. They sneak around in different disguises, popping in and out of your mind when you least expect it, and most of the time you might not even know they're there.

When you get to know these unwanted thoughts better, however, you discover that they steal things—like your attention, your energy, your hope, your self-esteem. And, like all pesky thieves, they keep coming 'round, if you don't consciously work to arrest them, reform them, and eventually set them free with your joy.

Whether you did these exercises or not (all work in this process is strictly voluntary!), they introduce a powerful tool that, in conjunction with the Enlightenment Exercise, will gracefully dissolve the tobacco habit.

The Enlightenment Exercise Revisited

Dr. Almayrac has used the Enlightenment Exercise and the journal-writing tool both personally and with his family and clients to heal successfully a wide variety of diseases, injuries, and illnesses, and to balance and uplift every type of personal, familial, and economic relationship.

Joy is *the sign of the active healing spiritual presence!*

In the first two chapters, you were introduced to the basic Enlightenment Exercise and its application to mastering smoking. To practice this exercise—to "play the game"—is actually very simple, very natural. In fact, most children do it all day long, every day. And because we were all children once, many of us still play along in one way or another, simply because happiness is our original nature as well as our long-term goal. We are not without inherent wisdom in regard to attaining happiness.

"Most people have a reasonably high opinion of themselves," observes Dr. David Myers, a sociologist who has studied happiness through extensive surveys across the United States. "And that fact in life goes a long way in explaining why most of us are, indeed, reasonably happy and satisfied with life."

When you think thoughts you enjoy about yourself, you necessarily have a reasonably high opinion of yourself, and thus you are reasonably happy. What happens when we start practicing the Enlightenment Exercise—consciously verifying that we are in fact enjoying each and every one of our thoughts and feelings—is that we become much *more* than "reasonably happy." Indeed, we become *unreasonably* happy. We become stupidly happy! Fantastically happy! And not just when the home team wins a football game, or when we have old friends over for a barbecue. We're happy waking up and going to bed and all the time in between, even waiting at a red light and pumping gas at the self-serve. That "unreasonably happy" state of mind is fundamentally different, for most of us, from what we've known throughout most of our adult lives, but, undoubtedly, it's exactly what we were looking for when we started smoking.

In a classic series of books, a young sociologist, Carlos Castaneda, tells of his meeting with Don Juan Matus, a Yaqui Indian shaman, or medicine man. Don Juan eventually reveals to Carlos that he has a "different description of the world" than what most people know. The medicine man's description included what most people know of the world, of course, but it did not end there. His view of the world was in fact much broader, deeper, more "electric," alive, transcendent, than what most people know of the world.

So, too, when you start practicing the Enlightenment Exercise you will discover a "new description" of the world, unlike what most of the people around you are currently experiencing. When enjoying your happiness, you are not in "opposition" to the standard, school-taught description of the world. Rather, you find yourself enjoying a world that is somehow brighter, livelier, friendlier than the world you knew prior to practicing this liberating process.

And such a view appears to you, not because you are narrowing your focus (as some might suggest), but because you are perceiving the world with less fear, less trepidation, less distrust, and thus are seeing it with an open mind, more clearly, more directly. With such an expansive view, your sense of the world changes, and similarly, naturally, your actions in and reactions to the world change. Your old habits, bound to what was your habitual way of perceiving the world, fall away naturally.

To effect this "change of view," however, you must "apprentice" yourself to your own inner joy, to your natural happiness. When you are willing to honor your joy, as Carlos honored the Yaqui shaman, you are free to learn the many lessons it has to teach you.

"What good is it to be a man of knowledge?" Carlos asked Don Juan.

"That you might live in the world with joy," Don Juan replied. Your natural happiness will guide you, step by step, toward a "mastery" of life, and you will become not unlike the "man of power" or the woman of power, who Don Juan suggests is the eventual destiny of every person. A power person operates with increasing freedom in all areas of his or her life. Such a person progressively incorporates more of all that is strong, beautiful, magical, and mystical about the human condition.

Some people, when introduced to the Enlightenment Exercise, immediately recognize its beauty and power and spontaneously begin practicing, playing, day in and day out, for the rest of their lives. For these, the Enlightenment Exercise is simple and obvious. It is an articulation, a simplification, of what they have been doing already, and so they pick it up at once. It is, after all, a very natural spiritual discipline.

For most of us, however, having accepted the education and culture that we have, embracing the Enlightenment Exercise requires effort. For us, thinking in this way—thinking only what we enjoy—becomes a learned discipline, one that generally begins with little pieces here and there, and then grows, with the help of books such as this, as well as tapes, lectures, and personal encounters with those who have lived in an enlightened manner for many years.

The Power of the Written Word

One of the most direct ways of learning and intensifying the enlightenment process is with journal-writing. Journal-writing is a process almost every student uses at one time or another, to a greater or lesser extent, first, because it's a powerful method to dislodge inner "blocks" and uncertainties, and second, because it's fun! The journal-writing process is enjoyable, and so is the peaceful, joyous afterglow that follows.

In its basic form, enlightened journal-writing is simply putting your thoughts and feelings on paper and practicing the Enlightenment Exercise with them. There are several advantages to writing out your thoughts. First, putting your thoughts on paper slows them down—slows you down—which gives you a chance to enjoy them more and thus enjoy yourself more. Second, putting your thoughts on paper moves them "outside" of you, which allows you to actually *see* what you are thinking. Third, journal-writing allows you to capture and *tame* those thoughts, which, if untamed, keep you smoking—keep you addicted. Journal-writing just makes the whole enlightenment process easier, more concrete, more sustainable. And it's good practice for what we ask you to do without paper all day, which is to enjoy all of your thoughts.

"Top Five" Review

At the beginning of this chapter you were asked to write down the ten most-unwanted thoughts that you habitually think about smoking. The easiest way to do this is simply to write down the first ten thoughts that come to mind—without censoring, without "analyz-

ing" or judging—just whatever comes to mind. For instance, the
first five on your ten most-unwanted list might be:

1. I shouldn't smoke.
2. I can't help myself.
3. Smoking is dangerous for me and for others.
4. Smoking is dirty.
5. Smoking is expensive.

These first five most-unwanted thoughts all appear to be negative,
which is not surprising since that's the atmosphere surrounding
smoking in our society. But the "unwanted thoughts" do not necessarily have to be negative. They might be positive—"I love smoking!" or "I'm so strong nobody's going to get me to stop!" But again,
positive, negative, or neutral makes no difference. What you're
looking for, trusting in, is your native joy.

So the thought, "I shouldn't smoke," popped up. To practice
the Enlightenment Exercise you simply ask yourself whether you
enjoy the thought, yes or no? You quickly perceive "No, I don't."
A perfectly honest, healthy, and efficient way to relate to this
thought is simply *not* to think it if you don't enjoy it. Just cross it
off the paper.

If you are strong enough, you won't think it again. "Oh yes,
I've crossed out that thought. I don't need to think it anymore."
You fortunate few don't need any additional thoughts to "arrest"
the thought, "I shouldn't smoke"; you just stop thinking that way.

But, for many, the old habit of thinking, "I shouldn't smoke,"
isn't an easy one to drop. So, what are three thoughts you might
use to arrest or counter that thought?

To give an example of how the exercise works, let's find some thoughts having to do with this particular mindset that you *do* enjoy.

You could write, "I *should* smoke!" Writing such a thought—politically incorrect and forbidden as it is—probably gives you a certain amount of pleasure or joy. So be it. If you enjoy thinking "I *should* smoke," more than you enjoy "I shouldn't smoke," then go for it! Go with the one you enjoy. You don't have to make it logical or rational, just joyful! "I *should* smoke!" If you're going to smoke anyway, this is a wonderfully supportive thought!

What's a second thought that would help arrest the unhappiness of that original thought? How about, "I shouldn't smoke if I want to live to be three hundred years old, like the yogis in India." That lifts the original thought just enough to allow you to enjoy it.

Here's a third thought to help arrest the unhappiness of the first thought: "I shouldn't smoke if I am going to play in the next Olympics or if I'm going to swim the English Channel."

I trust you see what we are doing here. We are changing our habitual thoughts—not to conform to our *railroad* mind, but rather to elicit our joy.

Such an approach may sound radical, or dangerous, or silly. It isn't. As far as your health is concerned, it matters little whether the thought you think is true or not. What matters is your *joy* in thinking it. Remember, enjoying your happiness is the most important thing for you and for everybody else. So if you don't enjoy the thought, "I shouldn't smoke," the first option in the Enlightenment Exercise is simply, don't think it!

You don't even need to think a thought that's remotely similar. Instead, you might write down something like "Fishing is going to be great this year!" or "I'm going to buy a new hat." Both of these thoughts are wonderful and sufficient replacements, if you enjoy them more. Whatever the new thought, it will help you change the habit of the old thought, a little bit at a time, one small step at a time. Or, if you are able to simply drop the old thought, that's fine, too. Either way is perfect!

Again, you are not trying to find a thought that is *more* true or real. Whether you should or shouldn't smoke is not the point. Your thinking, "I shouldn't smoke," simply does not help you *not* to smoke! (Haven't you been thinking, "I shouldn't smoke" for a long time? Has it helped you not to smoke? No! It's part of the habit of addiction. So just drop it, or change it!)

The strategy of this book is to encourage and help you to begin enjoying your life more—right here, right now—by enjoying your thoughts and feelings. Joy—a form of love—is what empowers you. It is the only path to true self-mastery. Enjoy your thoughts! Enjoy your feelings! That's the bottom line.

So you've crossed out the first thought and written something you enjoy more: "I'm going to win the lotto on Saturday."

Okay, let's move to the second thought, "I can't help myself." (In your own journal-writing, I know you'll be moving a lot faster than we are here!)

The same simple strategy could be employed with the second thought—if you don't enjoy it, simply cross it out, and don't think it. Maybe you'll always choose this option—simply not to think about smoking at all, since you don't enjoy your thoughts about it. Or, maybe your strategy will be that whenever a thought about smoking comes up that you don't enjoy, you'll just *drop* that thought immediately and think about something you *do* enjoy (whether you actually engage in the physical act of smoking, or not).

This is perfect and appropriate training for mastering smoking: Simply don't think about it! Enjoy some other completely unrelated thought instead. After all, most nonsmokers and ex-smokers don't *ever* think about smoking! Thus, by simply not thinking about smoking—not being disturbed by it, dropping all thoughts you don't enjoy about it—you'll be doing *exactly* what nonsmokers and ex-smokers are doing! So you can see that, yes, dropping all thoughts about smoking and thinking instead, "I should buy a new hat," is a perfectly legitimate, very healthy and efficient strategy.

That said, let's play with it anyway. What thoughts can we use to arrest the unhappiness of "I can't help myself." What would you enjoy thinking instead? Maybe you'll write down, "I *can* help myself. I can help myself to a cigarette whenever I want." Yes, okay. You can enjoy that thought. It's goofy, but you can enjoy it and that's what counts. Or, "I *can* help myself by enjoying myself." Anything that lets a little light in, a little joy in, is perfect. You don't have to walk a thousand-mile journey. You only need to take a single step: Enjoy yourself a little more.

To do that, you also can elect the second option, which is not changing the thought but rather "enjoying the thought that you didn't enjoy a moment before." Can you do that here? Sure! If you think, "I can't help myself," relax! Don't fight that thought—don't fight yourself. Instead, enjoy yourself! If you can't help yourself, what's the problem? In the second option of the Enlightenment Exercise, you think the same thought but without condemnation, without antagonism. You are free to enjoy *any* thought. Joy is the key.

When you practice the second option, as mentioned in Chapter Two, you may choose to make your thoughts smaller, larger, brighter, dimmer, a different color, a different pace. You are free to do *anything* to your thoughts so that you can smile again.

On to the third thought: "Smoking is dangerous for me and for others." Of course it is! You are free to follow the second option and enjoy that thought, enjoy the danger. You knew, even before you smoked your first cigarette, that smoking was dangerous. That's part of what made the adventure of that first drag so exciting. That's part of why you enjoyed it. Dr. Almayrac points out that some degree of danger is enjoyed in all cultures. In the United States, it might be auto racing, kayaking, bungee jumping, mountain climbing, roller-coaster riding, or even promiscuous sexual adventures or other forms of social risk taking. Danger in itself is not unenjoyable. So, if you can, you are free to enjoy the thought, "Smoking is dangerous for me and for others." You may even want to add: "We all die sometime!"

However, most of us are not accustomed to enjoying or welcoming such danger. So let's choose the first option in the Enlightenment Exercise—let's drop that thought and find one that might be more enjoyable. It can be a thought about anything ("I'll buy a new hat"), but for our purposes, let's keep it in the smoking section. You might write, "Smoking is dangerous, but *not* enjoying myself is even more dangerous." Perfect! Or maybe you'll write, "Joy is the safest energy in the world." Or, "My joy protects me and those around me." Or, "The cigarette I truly enjoy does not hurt me." Or "What hurts other people the most is when I don't enjoy them, don't love them." The possibilities are endless! Simply write what you most enjoy.

Again, you don't have to find the "perfect" answer, the "perfect" antidote to a thought you don't enjoy. You simply need to find a thought that you enjoy just a little more than the first one. And then another thought that you enjoy just a little more than the second, and so on. You begin where you are. If you are not totally ecstatic right now with your thoughts about smoking, you nevertheless try to enjoy them a little more than you did before you started practicing the Enlightenment Exercise. And the more you practice, the more you improve.

"Smoking is dirty" was the fourth thought. So you ask, "Do I enjoy this thought, yes or no?" and find that you don't enjoy that thought immediately, spontaneously. You might begin to enjoy it with thoughts like, "smoking is *earthy*." "Smoking *grounds* me." "Smoking is the *nitty-gritty* of life." (Puns can be joyful, too.)

When writing in your journal, record each of your thoughts, one at a time. You don't have to continue with a particular thought, or its derivatives, for any set length of time. Joy, again, is your "governor" in this matter. You might find only a couple of thoughts you enjoy better. Great! Then move on. Or, you might find a particular thought will elicit ten, twenty, thirty, or even more thoughts to enjoy. The more you practice—the more you write in your journal—the more thoughts you will find to enjoy. You will also find that, with practice, you can enjoy more quickly the thought that you didn't enjoy a moment ago. "Smoking is dirty"—"Yeah! Kids love to get dirty! I'm not going to fight it. I'm not going to be a stuffy adult. I'm going to be a kid and have fun!"

You might enjoy that thought for a moment. The next moment, you might enjoy the opposite, "I'm a clean and tidy smoker." Neither consistency nor logic is necessary, only joy. The more you enjoy yourself, the more "fundamentally" consistent and the wiser you become.

"Smoking is expensive," was the fifth thought. "Do you enjoy this thought, yes or no?" "No." Okay. What would you enjoy instead? "Compared to the national debt, my smoking's a bargain!" Or, "You can't take it with you!" Or, "For the pleasure I get, the price is cheap." Or, "Smoking's expensive, and so am I. We deserve each other!" Or, "I'm expensive, but I'm worth it."

Of course, the "right" use of money is always to enjoy it—whether you enjoy saving it or investing it or giving it away. When money is enjoyed in some way, it is wisely spent. When it is not enjoyed, it is not wisely spent. Any one of these thoughts might come up in the enlightened journal-writing process.

Journal Mechanics

The actual mechanics of journal-writing can be whatever you find most comfortable. In his training classes, Dr. Almayrac suggests beginning by simply writing out a number of thoughts—five to ten—as we just did. These first five or ten thoughts should be spontaneous, immediate, and written without self-censoring.

Next, review your thoughts, beginning with number one. Cross out or put a line through those thoughts you don't enjoy, and add a thought or two, or more, that you find more enjoyable. The first journal page might look something like this:

1. ~~I shouldn't smoke.~~
2. ~~I can't help myself.~~
3. ~~Smoking is dangerous.~~
4. ~~Smoking is dirty.~~
5. ~~Smoking is expensive.~~

I'll buy a new hat!

The Broncos will win!

I can help myself.

I can help myself to a cigarette.

I can help myself by enjoying myself.

Especially in the beginning, it is often helpful to give each thought a separate line. This slows you down and fosters the basic and necessary discipline of working with one thought, or one feeling, at a time.

As you spend more time journal-writing, the mechanics evolve naturally, so that eventually you write in the way that comes easiest and is most comfortable for you. In my own journal-writing, I often find myself writing one sentence after another, side by side, without the interruption of a new line. Most days I abandon the literal "crossing out," doing it quickly in my head, instead, because I'm anxious to move on to the next thought I am happy to think. Other days I feel I need to slow down, so I return to the basic process mentioned earlier.

Again, there are three principal advantages to journal-keeping:

1. Journal-writing slows down thoughts and feelings long enough for you to enjoy them in a way that you otherwise wouldn't.

2. Journal-writing helps to clarify your thoughts and feelings (especially about smoking) and makes them easier to enjoy.

3. Journal-writing forces you to confront (i.e., *"bring to the front"* or "look at") thoughts and feelings you may not have wanted to consider, thereby helping you to come to

terms and "make peace" with these thoughts and feelings, and, more importantly, with yourself.

In a word, you write in your journal in order to know and enjoy who you are. And, more particularly in this context, you write in your journal to untangle the web of thoughts and feelings that you don't enjoy and that keep you ensnared in the world of tobacco addiction.

Journal-Writing as Meditation

Enlightened journal-writing is a powerful form of meditation and self-discovery. It can also be a form of prayer. When you focus enlightened journal-writing on a particular topic, such as smoking, your experiences with it are absolutely and very quickly going to change for the better, because so much joy consciously is being focused on that topic. Even if you don't do the Enlightenment Exercise at any other time of day, your ten or twenty or sixty minutes devoted to journal-writing will produce a positive, noticeable effect on your mood that will last throughout the day.

To truly "master" smoking, you will need to evolve to a point where you enjoy all of your thoughts and feelings about smoking. You begin to do this informally, throughout the day, by internally employing the Enlightenment Exercise with all of your "smoking thoughts." To make this informal work even more powerful, more effective, you then perform the Enlightenment Exercise overtly through the journal-writing process.

As I said, focusing your journal-writing on one subject or area of your life is a powerful, useful, and efficient process. You can write about your job, your finances, your spouse, your kids, even your in-laws, and you'll find it clears the clogged drains!

Regular daily journal-writing, even without a particular intentional focus, is a very powerful way to bring new light to all areas of your life. You do this simply by writing down the first five or ten thoughts that come to mind, regardless of their topic. What's bothering you—what you are not enjoying—will quickly show itself. If you're "stuck," or having a problem, or irritated in an area not related to your "intentional focus" (for example, if you're mad at the boss, which doesn't have anything to do with your smoking), these thoughts are going to surface, and it's helpful for you to deal with them immediately. In this way, "general" journal-writing may be just as efficient, just as useful, in coming to master smoking as the "focused" journal-writing we've already discussed. As I've said before (may I not be harangued for pointing it out again!), the primary goal of this work is not to get you to quit smoking, but rather to help you enjoy your happiness more than ever before. As you become "unreasonably" happy, your smoking habit will fall away of its own accord.

Way back on page 42, when we suggested those first five unwanted thoughts about smoking, you probably did not find them particularly enjoyable, but you may not have felt unhappy or troubled by them, either. After working with them through this journal-writing process, however, even indirectly, just reading along, have you noticed that your basic sense of happiness, of "okay-ness," is more apparent, not just with those thoughts but in general? When you work with your thoughts in the journal-writing process, your natural happiness is magnified. The light of your joy burns much brighter!

"Enlightenment is your ordinary mind," as Huang Po said. This ordinary happiness, this ordinary "okay-ness," is the power we focus on and magnify throughout the book. Nothing special, nothing extraordinary, at least here in the beginning.

If you embrace this process and actually do the work, you will reach a point when you realize that you have been enjoying your ordinary happiness every day for weeks on end. After a while, and sooner than you may think, you will realize that you have become proficient with the Enlightenment Exercise, that while your daily life is starting to brighten, unclog, and speed up, you are also becoming more peaceable, feel more in control and relaxed than ever before.

In our sample journal-writing, the new thoughts suggested obviously were not deep or profound—just the first ones that came to mind. In journal-writing, when you slow down long enough to examine your own thoughts, to look for the ordinary happiness, which in fact is the basis for *every* thought, you start to enjoy yourself with a depth and intensity and consistency not ordinarily experienced with "mundane" thoughts like, "I shouldn't smoke," or "I can't help myself."

Finding the Time

"But," you might wonder, "who has time for all this journal-writing? For paying such attention to the mundane thoughts of life?" In moments of doubt, remember to ask "What is the most important thing for me and for everybody else?" If you don't devote time to your happiness, what are you devoting time to? If you don't have time today to find pleasure in the thought, "I shouldn't smoke," when will you enjoy it? If you're not going to enjoy the nitty-gritty of your smoking, what will you enjoy?

Dr. Almayrac "practices" or plays the Enlightenment Exercise all day, every day. Part of his practice is enlightened journal-writing, which he generally engages in for a minimum of one to two hours and often for three to five hours, even on the days when he gives public presentations and private sessions.

"I am a professional," he explained to me.

People pay me for my excellence in this work. So like a professional athlete who trains every day, or a professional musician who practices every day, I *train* with my happiness. I am much better at it now than I was last year, and last year, I was better than I had been five years before that. Every day I enjoy more and more, and better and better, all that I am, and all that God is.

Many people have noticed how simply being in Dr. Almayrac's presence is a joyful experience—there's a certain happy "buzz" in the air. When you enjoy yourself—all of your thoughts and all of your feelings—consistently, day after day, you fill your aura with light. Your very cells radiate joy. People can't help but get a "contact high" from you. Healings, large and small, take place in your company.

When you practice enjoying all of your thoughts and feelings, when you train yourself this way, it's only natural for you to find the people you are with more enjoyable. And the people you are with quickly pick up on this. We all intuitively sense how others think and feel about us. You most enjoy those people—indeed, you want to get closest to those people—who most enjoy you. After all, it's more pleasing to be with an enlightened person than with a grump.

This basic enlightened journal-writing—just like a daily shower—refreshes you and helps you to keep "clean" mentally. It washes away thoughts you don't enjoy, and keeps the process of enjoying your life in the forefront. Of course, enjoying your life is first an inner process. But by bringing it outside onto paper, slowing it down, putting it into a material form, you magnify and strengthen the interior work. You become more joyful. So find some time, and write in your journal!

Isn't This Just Positive Thinking?

I want to caution against the assumption that we are simply advocating positive thinking. Some, or most, of the thoughts you enjoy may indeed fall under what has traditionally been referred to as "positive thinking." But "Forgetting how to smoke" is not, in the final analysis, about thinking, whether positive or negative, and it's not really about smoking, either. It's about joy! Sometimes you enjoy thinking a positive thought. Sometimes you enjoy thinking a negative thought. But, sometimes you don't enjoy thinking a positive thought. A positive thought, without joy, is powerless as an insight.

In the examples I gave, you can see that the five thoughts were not what would normally be considered positive thinking. And yet, with the enlightened journal-writing process, we were able to enjoy all five thoughts and many other thoughts surrounding those five thoughts.

"I have been helped very much by the school of positive thinking," Dr. Almayrac said. He continued:

And I was myself a good practitioner of it for many years. But in my [medical] practice I found that some patients were very much traumatized by some parts of positive thinking. For instance, I might have a patient say, or write, "I love my body," which would seem to be a very simple, very helpful positive thought. Yet not every patient could enjoy that thought. In fact, some people were very sad when thinking that thought, or very melancholy or disassociated. Many thoughts that are considered to be "positive" are thoughts that many people could not enjoy thinking.

As a medical doctor, I learned that my first responsibility is to "cause no harm." I was not happy to ask my patients—to insist for my patients —to do something, or say something or write something that obviously caused them sorrow and suffering. So that is when I began to search for a higher way, a more efficient way. And that's how this enlightenment process came to be developed.

What Dr. Almayrac discovered was that the power of positive thinking was not, in fact, in the positive thoughts themselves but rather in the *joy that the thinker experienced when thinking those thoughts.*

A wonderful little story illustrating this truth was told by Robert Ferre, Dr. Almayrac's good friend and first sponsor in the United States.

When Robert was in high school, he decided to do a science project showing the effect of prayer on plants. He very carefully "controlled" his experiment by dividing corn seeds into two equal, separate piles; mixing potting soil and separating it into two equal piles; having two identical "planting" containers; and devising a system to make sure each received equal water and sunlight. Over the seeds of one container, Robert quietly prayed for a set time each day for a period of many weeks. And over the other container, for an equal amount of time every day, Robert filled the air with "blue obscenities."

Now, as I understand the story, in Robert's home such blue obscenities and their attending emotions were not normally allowed or heard. But since this was his science project, and he was, after all, proving the efficacy of prayer, his profanities were excused. This was, for him, undoubtedly a delightful release from childhood constrictions.

And sure enough, the seedlings in one container outperformed—outgrew—the other in a quick and obvious manner. But wait! It was the plant he cursed over that outperformed the plant he prayed over! What happened?

It was not until many years later, when talking with Dr. Almayrac about the power of happiness, that Robert finally understood what had happened in his "corn seed" experiment. Joy is the power of life. And joy is the power of prayer. "These things have I spoken unto you," said Jesus, "that my *joy* might remain in you, and that your *joy* might be full!" (John 15.11, emphasis added)

Exercise

If you haven't done it yet, try it now! Write down your ten most-unwanted thoughts about smoking. Then, write for each of the ten thoughts you do not enjoy, three wanted thoughts that you enjoy more.

Whether you did it at the first or here at the last, the suggested exercise for this chapter takes the inner, reflective Enlightenment Exercise into the physical world of paper and pen and makes it real. If you're still resistant, try writing down just five thoughts. See what the process feels like; notice how your thinking changes. Once you've started, I'm confident you'll discover, as I did, that enlightened journal-writing is an extremely powerful tool. You can literally write your way toward the realization of an absolutely joyful life!

Now that you know the basics of enlightened journal writing and how to apply it, informally and formally, in your daily life, wait until you see where it leads you and how it affects the other parts of your life—like eating, sleeping, going to work, and reading books!

In the next chapter, you'll learn how this joyful approach to smoking is the key that unlocks the mystery of nicotine and all of its seemingly paradoxical effects.

4 The Search for Nirvana

Why You Smoke, and Why Nicotine Is Not
Really Your Enemy!

Tobacco is a dirty weed.
I like it.
It satisfies no normal need.
I like it.
It makes you thin, it makes you lean,
It takes the hair right off your bean,
It's the worst darn stuff
I've ever seen.
I like it.
—G. L. Hemminger

It's time to explore some of the known facts about nicotine,
because in conventional stop-smoking programs it's not unhappiness (our focus) but *nicotine* that is cast as the villain one must battle to escape.

The Nature of Nicotine

From a strictly physiological and pharmacological perspective, it
has been assumed that nicotine is the cause of smoking addiction.
Nicotine thus is the culprit—the physiological drill sergeant, if you
will—that keeps you marching back, pack after pack, year after
year. Most scientific researchers assume that smokers smoke in
order to obtain more nicotine. "There is little doubt," wrote the

researcher M. A. H. Russell, "that if it were not for the nicotine in tobacco smoke, people would be little more inclined to smoke than they are to blow bubbles or to light sparklers."

We've all probably enjoyed blowing bubbles and lighting sparklers, but we are not compelled to do so—as we are with cigarettes—every twenty to thirty minutes through all our waking hours, day after day, year after year. If Russell were one hundred percent correct in his assessment of nicotine's role in tobacco addiction, however, then the nicotine patch and the nicotine gum and, the latest, nicotine snort (inhaler) would be one hundred percent effective in releasing all smokers from their habits. Simply put, the theory is that once you have enough nicotine in your system, you'll no longer feel like smoking. Clearly, this is not what happens.

Independent studies show that nicotine gum has, at best, a ten to fifteen percent success rate when used without any other program. On its own, the patch has, at best, a twenty to twenty-five percent success rate. Some studies, both of the gum and the patch, suggest a more modest success rate, ranging from five to twelve percent. Recently, the American Medical Association has issued warnings about the possibility of "nicotine overdose" for people who wear the patch yet continue to smoke, even if sporadically.

So what's happening here? With both the gum and the patch, nicotine levels in the bloodstream are supposed to be sufficient to neutralize any nicotine craving, yet still the smoker wants a cigarette. Obviously, the smoking habit involves more than a physiological-pharmacological ratio.

In my work with smokers over the years, some have opted to use nicotine gum, or the patch, or the inhaler, or one of the other "regulated nicotine injectors" during our work together. In my experience, these students have a success rate that approximately equals that of students who choose not to use a nicotine substitute. This has made it quite obvious to me that most smokers smoke regardless of their current nicotine levels. More specifically, smokers smoke in order to enjoy themselves!

Obviously, both the nicotine patch and the nicotine gum ("the gum tastes like you're chewing cigarettes," one friend reports) have helped many smokers move through that difficult transitional period between their smoking and nonsmoking lives. The smokers who used them successfully were ready to make the transition and these methods helped. Coupled with the conscious remembrance of happiness, which we offer in this work—these alternative nicotine products prove even more successful. For those who enjoy using these aids, please continue!

Do recognize, however, that nicotine is neither the good guy (in patch or gum or snort form) nor the bad guy (in tobacco form), as some might assume. Let me explain.

The Basics

You want to enjoy yourself in many different ways, all day, every day. We all do. That's natural. As far back as Aristotle, observers of human nature have recognized this basic desire, which is healthy. That's a big part of life on Earth. Not only do we want to enjoy ourselves, it's important that we do, for this connects us with our deepest spirit. Newborn babies who are not loved, cuddled, enjoyed, wither. The idea is summed up in the Law of Happiness: *Enjoying my happiness is the most important thing for me and for all those around me.*

For most smokers, nicotine is used as one of the primary paths to "repeatable happiness," even though they may no longer recognize that it functions in this manner. For some people, nicotine is the only way they allow themselves to enjoy their innate happiness daily.

Nicotine is a paradoxical, quite efficient, and—as millions of smokers have discovered—a routinely pleasant little drug, though the long-term side effects are most often (but not always) deleterious. As every smoker knows, however, in the short-term, nicotine has different and contradictory, most often *quite pleasurable,* effects. And these effects are different at different times of the day. The existence of these paradoxes has been documented scientifically by researchers.

For instance, when first entering the system, nicotine increases your heart rate. Further ingestion, however, *decreases* your heart rate. That's one of the reasons you want to have a smoke when you wake up in the morning and why you also enjoy having a smoke before you go to sleep at night. You're getting two different effects at different times of the day from the nicotine you're inducing into your system. (This is a versatile drug!)

Nicotine has a similar effect on blood pressure. At first it increases blood pressure, but with further use it causes the blood pressure to drop. Likewise, nicotine has a similar effect on the brain. While at one point it acts as a stimulant—enhancing the "communication" between synapses,° thus quickening memory

---

° Synapses are the junctions between two nerve cells. They consist of minute spaces across which an impulse—pleasure, pain, musical sounds, or cacophonous noise, for example—passes when prompted by the appropriate neurotransmitter substance.

and enhancing ability in the learning tasks, at another point (and in different experiments with different researchers and/or levels), nicotine *inhibits* the action of synapses, resulting in a corresponding decrease in thinking ability.

Research has been conducted on nicotine's impact on virtually *all* parts or systems of the human body, and in almost all cases, it invariably has similar paradoxical effects. Examples abound! Nicotine has the ability to stimulate the release of adrenaline, and at other times it has a contradictory soporific, tranquilizing effect. You smoke to pump yourself up, and you smoke to relax. At one point, nicotine excites the nerves in your muscles, and at another point it induces a mild paralysis in your muscles. Low doses of nicotine increase your breathing rate; higher doses slow down your breathing rate. Nicotine mildly blocks urine yet stimulates the intestines. And, even though your intestines are stimulated, digestion is slowed. And, even though digestion is slowed, saliva and mucus are increased.

Nicotine seems to be the proverbial "snake oil" that promises to do whatever it is you want or need it to do. Undoubtedly, this is why researchers at Maudsley Hospital, London, England, conclude, "Cigarette smoking is probably the most addictive and dependence-producing behavior known to man." (On the contrary, our own research has proven that there is a behavior more addictive than smoking: *thinking* what you most enjoy thinking! Once you get hooked on that process—enjoying yourself all day every day—you'll have no desire even to try to break the mental patterning.)

Nicotine is, in the single doses offered by one cigarette, a fairly mild drug. It's a gentle, pleasurable little drug that can take you up or down, in or out, left or right. That's why it's so popular.

It's not like heroin or acid or speed, which *zoom,* or *explode,* or *rush* through the body with exaggerated and volatile effects. Nicotine is more of a "middle class" drug—a "Sunday school" drug, which is often taken in polite company to moderate the ups and downs of daily life.

So here's another politically incorrect conclusion: Tobacco, nicotine, has been very efficient in helping you—and millions of people all over the world—to enjoy your life more by moderating your ups and downs. You were not—are not—"wrong" to desire the comfort which such moderation brings to you. You are not wrong to desire the pleasant physiological changes that nicotine causes. Such changes—such stimulation and numbing—are in fact quite useful and pleasurable. You are wise to acknowledge them and to admit your enjoyment of them.

Why Smoke?

A great deal of research has been conducted into why people start smoking in the first place and why they continue smoking the way they do. We'll talk in Chapter 7 about the many different reasons you might have had for starting smoking. (Statistics show that most of us start smoking *before* age eighteen, and many of us started before age fourteen!) You will also discover why and how the reasons you had for *starting* smoking will propel you to outgrow your smoking so many years later.

But for now, let's examine the primary reason for your smoking: You enjoy it! (Remarkably, this will be the same reason you stop smoking: You will enjoy *not* smoking!)

Most researchers claim that the reason you continue smoking is because your body needs and craves nicotine. However, what your body *truly* needs and craves is joy. Joy is the body's "mother's milk." In smoking, you've simply trained yourself to access your joy through nicotine. It's time to train yourself for wider access.

Researchers are often frustrated when they ask smokers why they smoke and discover that smokers frequently don't know how to respond. Most smokers aren't able to articulate why they keep smoking. And when smokers *do* come up with reasons explaining why they continue to smoke, their reasons, like the effects of nicotine, are quite contradictory and paradoxical. A common litany of reasons might include the following: "I smoke to relax.... I smoke to psyche myself up.... I smoke to be social.... I smoke to be alone. ... I smoke when I'm hungry.... I smoke when I'm full." Such conflicting responses seldom fit neatly into research models. And, traditional science is still reluctant to accept the possibility that the answer can be both "yes" and "no," or both "up" and "down"; "left" and "right." Nevertheless, when it comes to nicotine, such contradictory, paradoxical answers keep appearing.

The reason many smokers cannot articulate why they smoke—even to themselves—stems from the fact that the simple, true, and obvious answer (i.e., "I smoke because I enjoy it!") is taboo in light of our current cultural conditioning. Science and society tell us we should not enjoy smoking, and if we do, certainly this is no reason to continue.

When asked why they smoke, some smokers will admit they enjoy it. However, knowing consciously or subconsciously that society does not consider joy sufficient "cause" for doing anything, they quickly add reasons to justify their joy: "I enjoy it... because it makes me relax. Or, "I enjoy it... because it gives me energy."

Or, "I enjoy it...because it helps me concentrate." Whatever.

There's an easier way. To answer the question, "Why do you smoke?" with only the simple and obvious answer, "I enjoy it," allows you to approach smoking with a clear mind and honest heart. How refreshing! How empowering! You smoke because you enjoy it, period! That *is* reason enough. The courage to offer such an answer comes in recognizing the validity of the first step: Enjoying your smoking is the first step in enjoying not smoking. (If you still claim, "But I *don't* enjoy it," may I suggest that you do not yet understand your habit. If you did not truly enjoy smoking, you would not—and would have no need to—continue to smoke. You would naturally refrain from it. If you truly don't enjoy smoking, then give yourself a break: Don't do it any more! It's as simple as that. The most important thing for you and everybody else is to enjoy your happiness. If you aren't enjoying smoking, you'll find it's very easy to abandon.)

Your own happiness is the simple, ordinary energy that naturally transcends the various paradoxes of life itself: All the opposites, all the contradictions, not only in your smoking life but in every area of your life. That's why we call the process of discovering true joy "enlightenment."

Requiring joy, you are happy to be stimulated by nicotine when you wake up. You are happy to be tranquilized by nicotine when you go to bed. You are happy to use nicotine to concentrate and you are happy to use nicotine to let loose or relax. It is joy you are seeking in all of the paradoxical effects of nicotine.

Magnifying your natural joy, your innate happiness, therefore, is the single most perfect antidote to nicotine cravings. Happiness is what you truly crave! You've given yourself happiness through nicotine. Okay. Now is your opportunity to broaden the horizons of your happiness.

Your native happiness contains the only energy quick enough, strong enough, wise enough to move, step-by-step, with nicotine—to dance with nicotine—through all of its paradoxical and contradictory routines. Wherever nicotine wants you to go, for whatever reason, your happiness is already there. That's why your own ordinary happiness is the perfect remedy for tobacco addiction. It's simple, and it works.

And, of course, your natural happiness is available not only with nicotine. Your happiness remains available to you without nicotine, when smoking is not even a consideration. When you're doing something else, when you have forgotten to smoke, your natural happiness remains with you as your partner, your collaborator, your companion, your confidant. You can turn to your happiness in any circumstance: You can ask it advice; you can rely on it; you can relax with it. It gives you strength, wisdom, and the power to persevere.

So, again, if there is to be a "master" of nicotine, and of smoking in general, it is your own daily happiness that is best suited for the job. Happiness, joy, is the key to mastering the various effects, stimulations, and depressions of nicotine.

As mentioned earlier, nicotine in its own right is a fairly mild drug. The powerful addictive qualities attributed to nicotine are primarily due to the variety of pleasures the smoker associates with it. The paradoxical effects of nicotine allow you, the smoker, to decide whether to use nicotine for relaxation or for stimulation, for release or for concentration, for solitude or for social icebreaking. In other words, it is your joy (your enlightenment!) that determines what effect nicotine will have on your system!

You are already addicted to enjoying yourself! That's great! Now you just need a more efficient way to get your "fix" of joy. If you do the Enlightenment Exercise as consistently as you do your "nicotine exercise," you will quickly discover that it, too, is addictive, but in the best way possible.

When you are having a nicotine fit and can't wait to go have a cigarette, you are telling yourself—thinking to yourself—that you are unhappy with where you are, what you are doing, what you are feeling, who you are with, and that you would rather be in a more comfortable place. When you *finally* get to have a cigarette, don't you feel better with the first puff? Nicotine enters the system quickly, but not *that* quickly! You feel better with the first puff because you are finally dropping the thoughts you don't enjoy (e.g., "I need a cigarette, but I can't have one yet") and thinking what you do enjoy ("Ahh, finally...")

Similarly, you can relieve a nicotine fit by dropping the thought you don't enjoy and thinking a thought you do enjoy—even *without* nicotine! The "first puff of joy" is available to you always! It's not the nicotine that makes you uptight. Nicotine is mild, willing to bring you up or down. However, your thoughts about nicotine, about your smoking habit, about what you need to do to fix your unhappiness, are powerful, demanding, insistent.

As you practice enjoying your thoughts, dropping thoughts you don't enjoy, nicotine cravings spontaneously begin to diminish. By enjoying yourself, who you are, where you are, who you are with, what you are doing, you forget to smoke. (I've seen this happen in every class I teach!)

There are reports from all over the world of smokers who have stopped smoking without a single withdrawal symptom!

Although it is unusual, it is not uncommon. If you start asking ex-smokers about their withdrawals, you may discover a surprising number had no withdrawals at all. Why? How?

They enjoyed smoking. They enjoyed not smoking. Their joy overruled, or transformed, the expression of any negative withdrawal symptom. They were simply happy to be free of the smoking pattern, and their happiness was more powerful than the mild physiological effects of nicotine. On the other hand, when you are not enjoying your happiness—when you brace yourself for "the agony of withdrawal," and focus on those things that you are not happy to focus on, as most stop-smoking programs set you up to do—then nicotine will not disappoint you and you will likely experience difficult withdrawals.

In Chapter 11 we discuss specific (enlightened!) methods of dealing with withdrawal symptoms. For now, we simply want you to understand why nicotine is not the bad guy in this war, and why you can start right now to prepare for an easy, enjoyable "period of rebalancing" after walking away from tobacco.

Enjoying Tobacco: A Logical Way to Quit

It is well that man is logical. Because then he can create *reasons* for doing what he would do anyway.
—Benjamin Franklin

As a stop-smoking teacher, many nonsmokers and government health workers assume that I am part of the "anti-tobacco" armies currently invading the land. I repeatedly assure them that I'm not at war with smokers or tobacco—in fact I enjoy them both immensely! As mentioned, I see myself as a "refugee worker," working with the "refugees" of the tobacco wars.

Because of my work, I sometimes find myself at meetings of anti-smoking people. I am always amused by how frustrated many of these anti-tobacco people become, knowing that smokers, who know the medical facts about tobacco, continue to smoke. It seems so *illogical* to the anti-smoking people. Starting to smoke at all seems illogical to them. And continuing to smoke seems illogical, and wanting to quit and still not quitting seems illogical. Because they don't know what's happening in a smoker's inner life, they assume, logically, that nicotine is causing all the problems. (But, as we've seen, nicotine is *not* the logical solution to nicotine addiction.)

As we smokers and ex-smokers know only too well, cigarette smoking is not, alas, a logical behavior. But, like enlightenment, it's enjoyable and therefore quite compelling.

INSIGHT
Recall that since smoking is not strictly logical, you are not bound to approach its dissolution in a stintingly "logical" manner.

Of course, in the dissolution of the smoking habit, the power of logic is helpful. But logic in itself does not contain sufficient power to change your behavior. You already know that your smoking is not logical. Your own daily common sense tells you that. But your logic exercises very little power in your day-to-day smoking life. Here's why:

Even though your logic tells you it's not logical to smoke, you don't enjoy what your logic is telling you! And that is the key. Your joy is more powerful (and more necessary) than your logic! You may not be able to quit through the power of logic. You can—and will—quit through the power of joy!

You'll soon discover (if you haven't already!) that the enlightened approach is the most logical approach of all, and it is based on good old-fashioned horse sense.

So How Do I Logically Change My Ways?

Earnie Larson, in his cassette series, *The Transformed Self,* suggests that when you set out to change your personal habits, it is helpful to acknowledge that:

- There is no change without *understanding.*
- There is no change without *focus.*
- There is no change without *consistency.*
- There is no change without *accountability* and *support.*

Of course, some people do change their habits immediately and spontaneously, and no one knows why: There is no understanding, no focus, no consistency, no accountability or support. It just happens. That's life! It confounds even the experts.

Nevertheless, Larson's four criteria are indeed most often present, most often necessary, for those who want to change their personal habits. As Mickey Spillane wrote, "The race doesn't always go to the swift, but that's where you bet your dough."

So let's examine Larson's four criteria in relation to smoking.

1. *If there will be no change in my smoking behavior without understanding, what is it exactly that I should understand?* Understand that your own happiness—not this book, not your friends, not your doctor—will lead you to exactly what you need to be free of tobacco. Your own happiness will lead you out of the maze you've been wandering around in for so long. That's the most important thing to understand: Your own happiness is the key to your freedom.

The fundamental reason we smoke is simply because we enjoy smoking. The reason we want to quit is because we enjoy, at least a little, the idea of not struggling with smoking anymore. Understand that the easiest way in the world to quit is through your joy—your own ordinary happiness.

Understand?

2. *If there will be no change in my smoking behavior without focus, how exactly do I focus, and what do I focus on?* I bet you've already guessed the answer to this one! Right! Focus on your own feeling of happiness. Focus on those thoughts you enjoy. Drop the ones you don't. Your happiness is there, right now, this instant, as you read, because happiness never really leaves you. You may only feel a tiny little glimmer of happiness. Okay. Focus on the glimmer. It will grow!

You focus on your happiness by being aware of the thoughts you are thinking. Focus on one thought at a time. A good aid to focus is the question, "Am I enjoying this thought, yes or no?" The journal-writing process also helps you to focus. (See Chapter 3 if you want to review enlightened journal-writing.)

3. *If there will be no change in my smoking behavior without consistency, what is it that needs to be consistent?*

Be consistent at enjoying your happiness. As you learn to do this, you will gain mental, emotional, and physical energy sufficient to forget to smoke consistently.

4. *How about accountability and support?* You are always accountable for remembering your own happiness—no one else *gives* you your happiness or takes it away, although it may be influenced. Happiness is your inherent nature. You alone are accountable for remembering and relying on your native happiness, regardless of outside appearances or circumstances.

Although it is unusual in our culture, you will actually find great support whenever you remember and act on your happiness, because everybody has the same compulsion for joyful enlightenment. When you are genuinely happy, you spontaneously support other people in the way *they* want to be, which, of course, is naturally, natively happy.

When it comes to smoking, you may find it helpful to introduce other smokers to this program. If you choose this approach, remember that you are *not* primarily trying to help each other quit so much as you are helping each other *enjoy* who you are right now, so that quitting becomes a natural, easy, enjoyable thing to do.

Exercise

1. In your journal, begin collecting examples of the paradoxical reasons you smoke, in particular. Write down the paradoxical circumstances side by side (e.g., to wake up, to go to bed; when you're hungry, when you're full; when you're with company, when you are alone.)

2. For each of these circumstances, open yourself to the happiness—the joy—you were feeling, before, during,

and after you smoked. In other words, become aware of the little joys you were feeling in these moments.

Do you still think this whole smoking and stop-smoking business feels like hell?

If so, you're in luck! In the next chapter, you'll find a quick, fun map of the various hells, purgatories, and heavens—what the Buddhists call *bardos*—through which you as a smoker often travel. It'll be easier to move out of hell, through purgatory, and directly to heaven if you have a map.

5 The Holy Volcano
A Map of the Smoker's Mountain

> Notwithstanding the sight of all our miseries, which press upon us and take us by the throat, we have an instinct [joy!] which we cannot repress, and which lifts us up.
> —Blaise Pascal

If you decide to stop smoking and you are in a high state of consciousness at the time (which is where joy takes you!), your decision is then very powerful. On the other hand, if you decide to stop smoking and you are in a low state of consciousness, your decision has little power and is good for only a few hours (or minutes!).

As we learned in Chapter 4, you smoke for different reasons at different times throughout the day. But you also smoke for different reasons in different seasons of your life—at different ages and stages. Wouldn't it be helpful to know which stage you are in and to have a map with directions detailing the most direct route to the next higher level of consciousness? Moving through the levels of consciousness has traditionally been described as climbing a mountain. Since we're talking about a smoker's levels of consciousness, perhaps we could say we are climbing a volcano. In that case, the highest level—the "peak experience," we could say—is when we are face to face with God, Eternal Light, or the fire within.

Muslim mystics in the Sufi tradition, as explained by Oscar Ichazo of the Arica Foundation, have developed such a map of consciousness. The map is divided according to the *number of laws* that operate in each state, or at each level, of consciousness. The highest states of consciousness have the fewest laws binding them. The lowest levels have the most laws binding them.

In the following pages, you will be introduced to a map of the Smoker's Mountain, which is loosely based on the Sufi map of consciousness. The map shows the basic characteristics of various states of mind most smokers experience daily. For each state, we'll briefly examine what it's like to be a smoker at that level and we'll mention some stop-smoking strategies typical of each particular level. The levels on the Smoker's Mountain correspond to a smoker's consciousness and the intensity of the laws operating at each level. At the highest level, the law of love is the only law. As we progress toward love, or joy, the more earthly loves that bind us fall away spontaneously.

We begin with six ordinary, but nevertheless relatively "hellish," states of consciousness that are familiar to all of us. (Actually, we are *familiar* with all levels of consciousness, if only in a fleeting manner. Spiritual maturity comes when we are able to sustain the higher levels.) Next, we briefly examine the characteristics of the higher states and discover why quitting smoking from these levels is easier, more joyful, and spontaneous than attempting to quit in a lower level.

Our Earthly Levels of Consciousness

The Smoker's Pit: "It's Me Against the World!"

This is a relatively low level of consciousness, a somewhat neurotic thinking pattern that we all fall into at times. We're in the "pit"

I and the Father are One

◆ UNION ◆

◆ COMMUNION ◆
All I see—within and without—is light, love, divine bliss.

◆ EMOTIONAL DOMINION ◆
All my thoughts and feelings are always in harmony.

◆ PHYSICAL DOMINION ◆
My body is my obedient and loving servant.

◆ INSIGHT AND INTUITION ◆
I'm better than okay—I'm happy!
That's my nature. That's my power. I'm where I need to be.

◆ WISDOM ◆
I've enjoyed smoking, and Joy is always healthy. I'm okay.

◆ THE SMOKER'S SUICIDE ◆
I can't go on like this. <u>Something</u> has to change, big time!

◆ THE HERMIT SMOKER ◆
I don't want to talk to anybody. . . or see anybody. . . or be anybody.
Please! Just leave me alone.

◆ THE SMOKER'S THINK TANK ◆
I have some theories about smoking.
Let's talk. . . talk. . . talk.

◆ THE SMOKER'S PEDESTAL ◆
I'm hip when I'm lit. All the world loves me! I need sunglasses.

◆ THE SMOKER'S BARREL ◆
We smokers stick together. It's we. . . We. . . WE against the world.

◆ THE SMOKER'S PIT ◆
It's me. . . Me. . . ME against the cold, cruel world.

The Smoker's Mountain

when we feel separated from everything and everyone and just *know* that it is everyone else's fault. For example, if a fellow gets thrown into the city jail—say for drinking or overdue parking tickets—and feels no remorse, he's typically seething, mad at everybody for putting him there. Such a person is in the "pit," separated, alone, fearful. He stands alone against the whole world.

When we're in this level of consciousness and think about our smoking, we say things like, "I'm *going* to smoke, damnit! I don't care what anybody says. I *deserve* to smoke because I've had [I'm having] a rough life. People [places, things] have really treated me badly. So I don't care what the scientists say. I don't care what the family says. I don't care what *anybody* says! They just don't understand. Besides, it's my life, my body. Nobody's going to own me. I'm going to smoke till I croak, and I don't really give a damn what anybody else thinks or says." We've all felt like this, yes?

When we try to quit from this low level of consciousness, we do so because we are feeling separate, alone. This state of consciousness has much fear and anger associated with it. So we try to quit because somebody has made us mad, or because we're feeling cut off from the world, or because of our health, or because our family or job has made us feel isolated, angry. We're feeling fearful and reactive and want to quit smoking in order to escape. Generally attempts at quitting from this level of consciousness make us feel even more fearful, more frustrated and alone. Such attempts are rarely successful.

The Smoker's Barrel: "We Smokers Stick Together"

This is the "group-mind" level of consciousness—a little higher than the "pit," the separated level of consciousness, but still not luminous. It's "our gang" separated from "their gang." In 1659, when the Puritans hanged Quakers from a tree with hemp rope on the Common in Boston (or when any group commits violence against another, for that matter), the work of this separated, prejudiced "group-mind," or mob mentality is at work.

If we smoke while in this state of consciousness, we may feel like this: "A lot of us smoke. And we're good people—really good people. I *belong* to this group. Smokers are my people. The people I respect most are smokers—at least the ones I used to respect were smokers. We can't all be wrong. We're good people. We're real. We may not all be rocket scientists, but we're genuine, and we stick together. We keep up our commitments. We've made a pact to keep smoking because we're all part of the group." From the vantage point of the group-mind level of consciousness, those who quit smoking are somehow traitors, betrayers of the cause.

When we try to give up smoking from this group-mind level we naturally try to do so as a group. Two or three or more of us make a pact to quit. We take strength and support from the fact that our group is doing it—"I'm quitting with my partner or people from my company, or my club, or my church, or my stop-smoking class. We're all doing it together!"

This group approach can be a successful way to quit—in fact, any way can be successful, from any level of consciousness. The danger is that if one member of the group fails or backs out of the agreement, then the motivation to quit may diminish for one or more of the others: "We were going to do this as a group." Similarly, if a member of the group resorts to smoking at a later date, it may cause the same pattern in the others: "Bill's smoking again. I don't think I can hold out anymore."

Of course, if everybody keeps the pact, then it can certainly be an emboldening arrangement. The separated group-mind is just not very grounded, certainly not centered. Because success is dependent on and vulnerable to outside forces, the foundation is shallow.

The Smoker's Pedestal: "I'm Hip, I'm It, I'm Lit!"

In this state of consciousness, our egocentric qualities are recognized as genuinely valuable (which they are!), and pride in and recognition of our individual talents are at the forefront. We feel quite special, quite polished, especially when comparing ourselves to other people.

As far as our smoking is concerned, this is our "movie star" smoking persona. We feel incredibly cool, incredibly hip, smoking the way we do: "Nobody smokes as well as I do." We smoke because, basically, we are secretly (or, in our mind, not so secretly!) *better* than everybody else—richer or more sophisticated or more powerful or more insightful, or meaner, or *potentially* just as rich, sophisticated, powerful, cool, hip. We're the top—perfectly ripe—banana.

When we try to quit from this level of consciousness, we do so because we want to show the world how a cool guy quits, or a how an incredibly in-control lady can just walk away from tobacco whenever she feels like it. We believe we are so special that we can probably give the world a glamorous example of how to quit. And sometimes it works!

However, this is a tough state of consciousness to sustain, because, obviously, there's a huge universe out there, and our own ego, however inflated, is still vulnerable to occasional barbs and pricks of reality. Of course, we can quit from almost any level of consciousness, with almost any motivation, but false pride is generally a fickle collaborator in this process.

The Smoker's Think Tank: "I've Got a Few Theories . . ."

Life has a tendency to make thinkers, philosophers—or at least *chatterers*—out of us all, because, like a river, it keeps changing, getting deeper, wider, then shallower, narrower, then wilder, then more tame. We want to talk about it because it's hard to stay on that pedestal. The victories of our egos are quickly forgotten. Life changes all the time and that makes us start to wonder, makes us stop to think . . . and so we start to babble.

At this level of consciousness, the intellect, however well- or ill-suited, becomes king. In regard to our smoking, we come up with ever-changing theories and speculations about why we do it, who's at fault, where it all began, assuming that at some point we'll be able to figure it all out rationally, logically. And once we do, we assume, smoking will no longer be a problem. "I think I smoke because, you see, when I was a kid, I never . . . [blah, blah, blah]." Or, "Maybe it's the Oedipus complex that makes me . . . [blah, blah blah]." Or, "My job, my insecurities, my spouse, my kids make me . . . [blah, blah blah]."

In this level of consciousness, we justify our smoking through a verbal, intellectual approach. At this level, we tend to focus on our personal history, trying to find patterns, trying to fit various pieces together to determine what it's all about.

When we try to quit from this level of consciousness, we assume that our logic, buoyed by our intellect, is going to lead us to freedom and will give us the strength to become free. It might work. It can work. Millions of people have quit smoking, and many of them undoubtedly did it from this level of consciousness—thinking (and thinking and thinking) in a logical, intellectual way about smoking, and then using that logic, that knowledge to move on.

As we already discussed in Chapter 4, however, most of us have already experienced the limitations of logic. The intellect and logic are good subjects, but as king their limitations quickly become apparent. To quit this way, as the old song goes, "You gotta have heart ... lots and lots and lots of heart."

The Hermit Smoker: "Please, Just Leave Me Alone."

In this state of consciousness you feel that you have a size-10 soul that won't fit into your size 6 body. *Everything* makes you feel irritated, cranky. Your job, your spouse, the kids, the dog, the color of the carpet make you want to have a drink, a smoke, a hit of one drug or another, or maybe more sex—something, *anything*, to release the anguish caused by the world of forms, the day-to-day, 3-D reality.

Many smokers often find themselves struggling with this relatively high state of mind. And it is a fairly high state, even though it feels low. The feeling is: "Please—I just want to be by myself. I want to decide on my own when, where, and how I'll stop—*if* I stop, which I'm *not* saying I will. Please, just leave me alone. I don't want to talk about it." And you don't want to think about it, either. In this level of consciousness, it's nobody's business but your own. When we try to quit from this level, we generally assume the best way to do it is to get away, by ourselves if possible, maybe up in the mountains in a cabin, or out in a boat, or at home behind closed doors when the rest of the family's going to be away.

This is a relatively high level of consciousness because the transient nature of form—all form, including one's own mortal existence—is becoming apparent, even though the solution to such transiency is not yet obvious. When we arrive at this state, we begin to look (or have been *forced* to look) at the deeper issues of life, like sickness, old age, and death. The question of smoking or not smoking becomes an irritable reminder of our existential condition. It makes us cranky.

Again, the success rate of those who quit from this level of consciousness is undoubtedly higher than the rate of those who try to quit from lower levels. (Remember, the higher your state of consciousness when you decide to quit, the more likely you will succeed.) Still, being a hermit with a size 10 soul and a size 6 body is a hard row to hoe.

The Smoker's Suicide: "I'm Dead Already. I Might as Well Do It."

There's a level of consciousness, right before "breakthrough," in which you are ready to do anything—anything at all—to effect a fundamental change in your life. Not only in relation to smoking— it might be with your job, your spouse, your health, your wealth. In this state of mind, you're tired of the ceaseless struggle. Tired of the war. Tired of the way things are and you just want out—you want out now. The hermit leaves his cave, ready to wreak havoc.

This is a relatively advanced state of consciousness because it reflects an awareness that we are more than our physical forms, we are more than a daily job, a comfortable relationship, a steady breathing in and breathing out. In our souls we know. We are infinite spirit, infinite happiness, dynamic creative beings, and to settle for anything less is itself a form of suicide. We want to bring an end to the false self, and we are ready to act on that desire.

In our smoking lives, we reach this state when we give up trying to quit. We are ready to "kill off" our urge to quit. We see that urge as a false urge, and we are ready to simply be honest, straightforward, totally accepting our smoking selves. "I can't quit. I give up. I'm going to eliminate every urge toward something other than what is right here. I'm quitting this quitting game. I'm smoking till I die."

Often it occurs to us that the easiest way to "quit quitting" is, paradoxically, to actually *do* it—to quit smoking. When we try to quit from this state of consciousness, we do it with the intention of "killing off" everything that has gone before. We're going to eliminate that old smoking self, that person who wants to continue. This state of mind is what leads us to throw the smokes out the window, or tear them up, to lash out at our family, to beat ourselves up mercilessly.

Again, it is possible to quit from this mindset, but it's a hard state to sustain. Generally, we either break on through to the more enlightened states, or, more habitually, fall back into one of the previous states. The efforts to quit from this state are fairly sporadic.

These six states of consciousness and various combinations of them are what most smokers who pay no attention to higher thought consistently experience in their ordinary daily lives. Although we are all familiar with these states, the fact that you are reading this book suggests that you are at least open to and curious about a higher way of being. In fact, you may already be practicing a more enlightened approach to your life.

As you begin more consistent practice of the Enlightenment Exercise and also do some form of daily enlightened journal-writing (see Chapters 2 and 3, respectively), you will discover that more and more you experience life from the vantage point of the higher states of consciousness.

Our More Heavenly Levels of Consciousness

Wisdom

Sooner or later the light dawns, and we realize that life is more than surface appearances, more than sense gratification, more than consumer victories or survival of the richest. We sense that something higher, brighter, more expansive than the narrow, fleshly outworking of our own personal destiny is happening here. It dawns on us that we're a functioning part of a larger, quite wondrous mystery. We sense that we are fundamentally spiritual beings. This realization is the beginning of wisdom.

Recognizing our spiritual (joyful!) nature, we cease to identify ourselves solely as smokers. This is wisdom. Sure, maybe we have smoked, maybe we are smoking, maybe we will smoke in the future, but we move into a level of consciousness where we no longer identify ourselves only that way. We begin accepting a more immediate, broader identification of ourselves as spiritual beings.

When we try to quit from this level of consciousness, with wisdom, identifying ourselves as spiritual—or at least joyful!—beings, we find it much easier. Through such wisdom, we gain a broader, more powerful sense of our abilities, of our inherent nature, and thus we gain confidence in who and what we are, and in who and what we are becoming. Setting aside cigarettes is simply one step along the enlightened path.

Insight and Intuition

As we live with wisdom, our insight and intuition mature. We look back on our lives and understand things we did not understand before. We look into our lives and intuit beauty where before we saw trouble. We look ahead and sense that the outworking of harmony is an immutable law, as surely as spring follows winter and sunshine follows rain.

When we function in this level of consciousness we may still smoke (we are more and more free of shoulds and shouldn'ts), but we are no longer conflicted about it. We smoke only those cigarettes (or pipes or cigars or chews) we enjoy. We do so with humor and lightness, consciously, deliberately, without guilt.

Similarly, when we decide to quit from this level of consciousness, we do so, with lightness and humor, intuiting the right time and place and method to make it easy, graceful, for ourselves and those around us. From this level, our insight into our own natural happiness is strong and clear, and we use this happiness to buoy us through the quitting process. We do it simply, cleanly.

Physical Dominion

We now move into levels of consciousness most of us have experienced only briefly, serendipitously, generally not because of conscious intention or true understanding. (Practice joy and these states spontaneously happen!) At this level of consciousness, you have conscious control of the physical body, including your autonomic nervous system, the functioning of your internal organs, your blood flow, among other thing. This is the state of consciousness a Hindu fakir utilizes when buried for six weeks with no food and little air. Demonstrations of fire-walking by popular self-actu-alization teachers show that anyone can be taught to sustain this level of consciousness, to some degree, for at least the time it takes to walk the coals.

Do we smoke at this level of consciousness? It's possible but not likely, simply because while in this state the conscious aware-ness of the body itself is so intense, so wondrous, so pleasurable and powerful that the idea of inhaling tobacco smoke just does not come up! We truly *forget* to smoke!

Quitting from this level of consciousness is, therefore, some-thing that happens spontaneously because we are so enraptured with the beauty of our inner and outer experience. Quitting smok-ing from this level is generally not a conscious decision. Rather, it's a natural omission of smoking—a "done deal"—that we realize only after it happens.

This state of consciousness is not as foreign as it might seem. At some deep level, you do have the potential to control all of your physical expressions, including the systems of your physical body. For most of us, this control is subconscious—we don't consciously cause our heart to beat, after all—but it is nevertheless a part of our individual expression. As we consciously open ourselves to our inner happiness, "that which is hidden shall be revealed." The true test, however, is not in the control of our physical body, but rather in the control, the maintenance of our happiness.

Emotional Dominion

In *The Path to Love,* Deepak Chopra suggests that each one of us, as infants, knew with certainty: "I am completely loved. I am com-pletely lovable." He believes that our walk here on Earth is to recover this sense of ourselves and to add one more: "I am completely loving."

This is the state of consciousness in which, no matter where we are, who we are with, what we are doing, or how difficult or easy the outer circumstances, we remain immersed in love, in happiness, in spiritual reality. We can express this love in an infinite number of ways, with any of the human conveyances of love that accompany our fleshly travels. We can fix flat tires, mow the lawn, drive the kids to school. But in this state of consciousness, we never lose sight of or contact with the underlying bliss that is the nature of life itself.

Even while smoking, it is possible that we have tasted this state at least briefly. Most of us have not learned to sustain it, to live in it, to be it. However, it is not unfamiliar to us because it *is* our essential nature.

Quitting smoking is the *result* of this state, because here our pleasure originates within; it is constant, overwhelming. The saintly, when in this state, often have to be reminded to eat, to dress. Smoke? Who can remember to smoke in the presence of such bliss?

Communion

In this mystical state of consciousness, form itself dissolves, or becomes transparent, and light is all, inside and out.

This state is not as rare or unfamiliar to us as we might at first suppose. For instance, we sometimes approach this state when we are with friends and have been completely carried away by laughter. For a fleeting moment, the world and everything in it, all we are, inside and out, is glee. For most of us, it lasts but a second, as we quickly impose form and circumstance and language on that glee.

We sometimes approach this level of consciousness in moments of quiet and solitude, when we have lost ourselves in peace, prayer, reverie; when, for a moment, nothing exists except calm. We are habituated to applying form and words and "things" to such states of consciousness to make them more familiar and useful to us. But we all have known moments when everything, inside and out, is one and beautiful.

In this state, smoking or not smoking is not a matter for consideration. *Being* itself is all there is. There's no one present to give up smoking, and there is no one present who is motivated to smoke. Life alone is here, and we are one with its galactic, atomic swirlings. All is bliss.

Union

When Jesus said, "Anyone who has seen me has seen the Father" (John 14.9), this is the level of consciousness he implied. There is no longer a *communion* between inner and outer, higher and lower, form and formless, I and Thou. There are no longer two to commune. Rather, there is one.

Ahh, home again!

William James, one of the founders of modern psychology, observed,

Our normal waking consciousness is but one special type of consciousness, whilst all about it, parted from it by the thinnest of screens, there lie potential forms of consciousness entirely different. We may go through life without suspecting their existence, but apply the requisite stimulus and at a touch they are there in all their completeness.

The "requisite stimulus" to change from a lower to higher state of consciousness is joy. The "requisite stimulus" to *sustain* this higher state of consciousness is also joy.

Joy is free. Joy is the "transcendental energy" that is unlimited, in both time and space. So no matter where you happen to be on the map, when you access joy, you immediately move toward the higher dimensions, the higher states of consciousness. And in the process, you spontaneously begin moving out from under the "laws" that would have bound you to the moment's circumstance.

That is the essence of the enlightenment process, which without fail will free you from the "rule" of tobacco!

Exercise

1. Practice enjoying everything in your life, all day, every day, inside and out.
2. If you can't do the first exercise perfectly, simply enjoy the fact that you can't do it perfectly and just enjoy the best you can!

Now that we have explored a variety of earthly and heavenly states of consciousness, you're probably wondering which state is for you in your particular situation and how you might go about attaining that state. That's what we are about to explore in the next chapter.

6 Be (Who You Are) Here Now
Why Right Where You Are Is the Perfect Place for You!

> Quiet [joyful] minds cannot be perplexed or frightened, but go on in fortune or misfortune at their own private pace, like a clock during a thunderstorm.
> —Robert Louis Stevenson

Don't worry about where you happen to be on the map of consciousness. Just relax. Where you are is perfect.

Are you a three pack a day smoker? That's *Perfect!*

Are you a once a week smoker? That's *okay!*

Has the doctor just told you to quit, for health reasons? *Perfect!* You're in great health? *Perfect!*

Are you recently married or recently divorced? Do you have a new job or an old job? Have you just moved? Were you just widowed? Just bankrupted? Just bankrolled? *Perfect!*

No matter what your situation is, right now, here today, you are perfectly suited to begin enjoying yourself, to use this book, and the exercises offered, and the approaches suggested in your journey toward (and in) enlightenment and freedom from tobacco.

Paramahansa Yogananda, in *Autobiography of a Yogi*, wrote:

A new student occasionally expressed doubts regarding his own worthiness to engage in yoga practice. "Forget the past," [his guru] would console him. "The vanished lives of all men are dark with many shames.

Human conduct is ever unreliable until man is anchored in the Divine. Everything in the future will improve if you are making a spiritual effort now.

That is, you don't have to *become* somebody different before you enjoy yourself. You don't have to struggle out of one state of consciousness into another before the burden drops away. You don't have to be more intelligent, more willing, more open, or more impressed than you already naturally are. Who and where you are right now is fine. Your only obligation is simply to *be* who you are. As you are. Where you are. "The ground upon which you stand is holy ground" (Exodus 3.5).

Your natural, ordinary state of mind is the basis for enlightenment. It is the basis for freedom. You always start from right where you are.

In the late 1960s, Richard Alpert, an ex-Harvard psychologist who had taken the spiritual name Baba Ram Dass, wrote a classic spiritual self-help book titled, *Be Here Now*. In this book, which deeply influenced a broad spectrum of counterculture baby boomers, Ram Dass detailed his own journey toward enlightenment, including his experiments with Harvard colleague and LSD guru Timothy Leary, and his eventual meeting and devotion to the Indian sage and miracle worker, Neem Karolie Maharaj.

"You don't need to go anywhere else to find what you're seeking," Ram Dass wrote. Where you are, right now, right here, is exactly where you need to be.

He went on to explain that you are, in fact, never anywhere else but right here, and that it is never any time but right now, even though you may habitually lose yourself in daydreams or wispy thoughts of other times and other places, both past and future. Ram Dass points out that you always have these dreams, these thoughts, right here, right now. In fact, you can never escape right here, right now. The injunction to "be here now," then, is simply a call to reality, a call to come home to the truth of being, to the way things really are.

To decide to enjoy your life right here, right now—to place your attention on what you are thinking right here, right now—is a high consciousness decision, a high consciousness way of living. You do not "abandon" anything by such a decision. Indeed, such a decision indicates that you are attuned to the wider reality, that you are attending to the truth of existence. When you are consciously "being here now" by paying attention to, and exerting mastery over, the thoughts you are thinking right now, life's power (joy!) infuses you. You are rewarded with more psychic energy, more emotional energy, more physical energy.

Be Smoking Now!

So in relation to smoking and the Enlightenment Exercise, what does it mean to "be here now"? Two things.

First, it means that when you smoke, you smoke consciously, here now, and not off somewhere else. You agree to "be here now" with your cigarette, enjoying it, not denying it, or pretending that you aren't really smoking, or ignoring your pleasure.

In the high state of consciousness—in the joyful state of consciousness!—you are not afraid to give yourself fully to whatever you are doing in the moment. If you are smoking, then that's what you enjoy. If you're not smoking, then that's what you enjoy. Being here now means that you're not trying to be somewhere else or to enjoy somewhere else other than where you are right now.

So that's the first thing: When you smoke, smoke. When you don't smoke, don't smoke. Be here, there—wherever you are—now, in the moment as you live it.

Second, it means that whenever you think about your past smoking behavior, you do so—right here, right now—with *joy*. As you've learned by now, this is the most healthful, most liberating way to think about your past behavior, not only for you but also for everybody around you. Thinking about your past history with present joy is adhering to the Law of Happiness. (See Chapter 2 for a reminder.)

"But I have a very abusive past," one drug addict told Dr. Almayrac when this suggestion was made in a public presentation. "I was very abused, physically, emotionally, and mentally. Are you telling me I should enjoy my past?"

"Yes, I am," Dr. Almayrac said.

"I don't see how I can possibly do that," the man said. "I don't see how can you even suggest it? If you only knew . . ."

"I know," Dr. Almayrac said. "I, too, at one time, had such a past. But now I don't."

"What do you mean, 'now you don't'?" the questioner persisted. "What's past is past. It's dead, gone. You can't change it."

"No. My past is alive," Dr. Almayrac said. "Whenever I think about my past, it is what I am thinking here, now. This moment is alive. As I change my thoughts, in this moment, about my past, my past changes."

Dr. Almayrac went on to explain some of his personal history and how his abusive relationship with certain family members was completely changed, moved to a new foundation, when he began changing his thoughts in each moment. It took him several years—during which he did not see or visit these family members. But when the work was done, the past had been healed, and joy—love—became the true basis for their relationship.

Dr. Almayrac does not suggest that people must "heal" all of their family relationships in the same way or form that he has done. (Today, Dr. Almayrac has ongoing relationships with all of those from whom he was once estranged.) He does suggest, however, that every relationship in our lives be filled with joy, with happiness, and that it is never too late to heal any relationship, even if someone is no longer in touch or has died.

With regard to smoking—which is a much easier history to heal than some other aspects of our personal lives—most of the people I have worked with have smoked all of their adult lives: ten, twenty, thirty, forty years or more. If these smokers were instructed to think of as "bad" what they have been doing for the past thirty or forty years, how much positive life energy (joy!) would they get from such an attitude? There can be *no* value or gain from thinking about your smoking history with chagrin. I encourage my students to honor their smoking histories because we are empowered, strengthened when we honor our previous life decisions. In addition, such mindset gives confidence and integrity to new decisions. When we acknowledge our smoking histories, we are free to assume that each of us did gain something from smoking—something good, valuable, necessary for that time, that place. We need not condemn our years of smoking. We are free to think about our years with joy.

Unlikely as it might seem, as we consciously "modify" our histories in this way—bringing the joy of the moment to the thoughts of the past—we find ourselves more and more free of those histories. However, if we begrudge and complain about our past, condemning ourselves as stupid, or juvenile, we lock ourselves into repeating the past, or a newer, more negative, version thereof.

Happy Quitting Memories

Not only should we enjoy our history of smoking and our present smoking (or nonsmoking!)—here, now—we should also enjoy our history of trying to quit smoking.

A study by researchers at the University of Ottawa, Canada, discovered that the majority of smokers who quit successfully do so only after having tried to quit and failing three to five times previously. The chances are that you have also tried to quit and have failed on numerous occasions. (If you were trying to quit because of fragmented, fearful, and unhappy impulses, you were wise to return to what you enjoyed. Your inner wisdom led you to do what was best for you and for those around you at the time.) Look at your previous attempts at quitting with humor, love, and devotion. Your past attempts were learning experiences, happy signs of life! Indeed, they were signs of your desire to move into a higher state of consciousness.

The failures? I encourage you not to view these past experiences as failures, but as *adventures,* learning forays into places you wanted to go. The paths you took were perhaps overgrown, difficult. Enjoy how far you traveled, and let it go. Perhaps you managed to quit for only a day, or a week, or a year (or an hour!) and then found yourself smoking again. You need not feel badly or discouraged because of this experience. But next time, take a different path!

"I had quit for four years," one of my students told me. "Four years! And then I started again. Can you believe it? What an idiot!"

I assured her she was *not* an idiot. My sense of it was that she had given herself a sabbatical, a vacation from smoking, but that she apparently still needed to enjoy herself through tobacco for one reason or another, or that she did not enjoy herself as much as she might have during those four years. Her lessons in joy with tobacco had not been completed, so she took it up again.

What If I Goof up Tomorrow?

When you admit that you enjoy smoking, and you determine to rely on your inner joy as a guide to the best path to take—here, now—to work your way free of smoking, your unhappy motivations, fears, and anxieties will become apparent to you. Recall, however, that because you are relying on your happiness—here, now—the old unhappy patterns no longer have power over you.

For instance, when a smoker tries to quit but then quickly abandons the project, it is often not because of something that is happening here now, in this minute, but rather because of thoughts of what *may* happen soon, somewhere else. We never fail by living—enjoying ourselves here, now—but rather because we abandon, at least in our thoughts, the here and now for the uncertain future. "My life has been full of tragedies and misfortunes," Mark Twain wrote, "most of which never happened."

Often, we "quit" quitting when we start thinking about what it's going to be like not to smoke *when*—when we're with our old smoking friends, or when we have our first cup of coffee, or when we're at summer camp, or ... all of those future times when it may be tough to be without a cigarette. Clearly, thinking about when it is going to be tough without a cigarette makes being without a cigarette hard right now. In a word, thinking about when it will be tough is thinking what we don't enjoy thinking. (See the Law of Spontaneity in Chapter 2.)

Be *here* now.

Or, on occasion, we determine to quit and then start thinking about all of the times we have smoked in the past, all of the different places. A five- or ten- or forty-year history comes up, and it starts to weigh on us, and we don't enjoy those thoughts about the past. It seems too tough to fight all those years, to go against the unhappy momentum of those years. So we have a smoke.

Be *here* now.

Do you ever wonder, or worry, what it's going to be like to be a nonsmoker? Relax. Be *here* now.

Do you wonder how you can explain your quitting to your old, disbelieving smoking friends? Again, relax. Be *here* now.

Do you worry that it might get *really* tough in a day or two, or in a week or two? You don't enjoy that thought—drop it. Be *here* now.

How Do I Do It?

The moment is eternal. It contains all of the past and all of the future because it contains your thoughts. Your thoughts are indeed timeless, free. Or, more exactly, your thoughts come from that place deep within you that itself is timeless, free.

As you become conscious of your thoughts and enjoy them here in this moment, right now, you begin to reside in the place within yourself that is timeless, eternal, infinite. You can go anywhere in the universe by means of your thoughts. In your thoughts, you can be with anyone, you can do anything. This is the nature of eternal consciousness, of *satchitananda*.

Your joy is not a thought. Your joy is that from which your thought arises and that to which it returns. Your joy is not a space. Space is that which comes out of joy. As you return to joy, as you return to happiness, you return to the truth of your life, the deep, abiding truth that sets you free from all time–space limitations.

So how do you practice "being here now?" Are you not supposed to plan for tomorrow? Are you not to enjoy your yesterdays? Are you supposed to abandon all destiny, all future, all past, and, *carpe diem,* seize the day?

Yes, that's exactly the way. Ease up on your plans for tomorrow. Let go of your yesterdays. Forget, for a bit, about your future. Take this tact at least a little more than you have in the past. You *can* live for today, live *in* today. You can enjoy your daily life. You can be more pleased and content with your daily experiences much more than you ever dreamed possible. You don't always need to live for tomorrow. As you begin living your life, honoring and enjoying your life here today, you discover that you are greatly empowered.

Our contemporary culture teaches us that the most important thing for ourselves and for everybody around us is to produce enough to make tomorrow's life better than today's. In our anxious striving to be so productive, we often lose the joy of today. And, in the process, we often lose ourselves, our love, our passion for living.

Paradoxically, when we begin prizing enjoyment, happiness (one thought at a time), over productivity—surprise of surprises!—our productive capacity increases. As we begin to enjoy what is here today, our tomorrows become more secure, more enjoyable. The means and the ends are the same.

When it comes time for the grave, the only thing you can take to the other side of the veil is your love, your joy, your "learned capacity for wonder." These are the treasures you lay up in heaven.

Your smoking life, your *real* smoking consciousness, in conjunction with your larger life pattern, has for one reason or another led you right here, right now, to this book, this chapter, this page. One of the spiritual laws of the universe says that because God is omnipresent and omnipotent, you need not go anywhere other than where you are to find what you are seeking. It is always available to you, within your own consciousness, right here, right now.

At this moment, you are neither "too enlightened" nor "too endarkened" to be able to use your joy and this book to guide you gracefully out of tobacco addiction. You are at the right place, at the right time.

As we briefly discussed in Chapter 5, the highest state of consciousness is an eternal consciousness, beyond time and space. These higher levels of consciousness are no more "acquired" than the summit of a mountain is "acquired" when climbed successfully. The summit already exists as you climb your way toward it. So too, the "summits of consciousness" already exist as you move from one level to the next.

How do you do it? By enjoying where you are, right here, right now.

And then again, right here, right now.

And then again, right here, right now.

Where else is there? What other time could it be?

Exercise

1. In your journal, write down a brief description—a few sentences—of the last three times you tried to quit.

2. Now write down three things you enjoyed about each of those experiences.

3. If you can't think of three things you enjoyed about each of those experiences, or even if you did, make up, imagine, three things you would have enjoyed if the experience had gone differently, and write them down (i.e., re-invent your life, rewrite your personal history!).

Now that we have explored the wisdom and pleasure of being here now, it's time to take a look at how the past and the future gracefully come together to liberate us—here ... and now.

7 Why Alpha = Omega, or The First and The Last Are the Same

You Were Happy (and Brave!) to Start Smoking!

> As above, so below; as within, so without. As it was, so it will be.
> —Revelation 16.5

You already know how it feels to think what you are happiest thinking. Even the grumpiest of grumps on occasion thinks those things that make him or her happiest. However, most children, unencumbered by education, do it all the time, spontaneously, effortlessly, because happiness is the native state of consciousness for every human being.

Think back, if you will, to the days and weeks and months when you first started smoking. Indeed, think back to the first time you ever smoked.

Exercise

Just for the fun of it, in your journal briefly describe:

1. The first time you ever smoked. What were the circumstances? Where were you? Who were you with? What brand of tobacco did you use?

2. When you first started smoking regularly. What were the circumstances? Who were you with? How did you feel? Give yourself the pleasure of writing a brief chapter about

your life, about when you first started smoking and the places and people involved.

As you examine the people and the events connected with your first smoking adventures, do you remember that you were happy to begin thinking of yourself as a smoker? Let the memories come back. Indulge yourself for a while. Didn't smoking feel bold and adventurous? Wasn't it a new and exciting identity to assume? Of course! Following your happiest thinking is always that way.

Even if you started smoking because of pressure from your friends, or from people you hoped would be your friends, or from your lover or someone you hoped would be your lover, even if you were the rare exception and were not truly happy to think of yourself as a smoker, you were nevertheless happy to think of yourself as one of the group, or one of the gang, or whatever it was that prompted you to smoke.

We all started smoking by thinking what we were happiest thinking.

Isn't it obvious that we can move out of a behavior by practicing the thought patterns associated with that behavior? Of course! In this context, the means and the ends are always the same. In fact, abandoning those first thought patterns—that original joy—is how you became trapped. So, if you haven't started yet, begin thinking what you are happiest thinking about for each area of your life, including smoking history.

In my classes there is usually someone who objects to this notion. Such a person might say, "I was feeling very lost and alienated when I first started smoking." Or, "I was going through a terrible family situation," or "I was trying to impress somebody." Or,

"I was with people who were no good for me." Our past is alive and here with us. How we *think* about the past—in this moment—is as powerful an influence on our lives as the so-called reality of the past. Still, the fact remains that we tend to do—indeed, almost always do—what we believe will make us happy.

When I question people who claim they started smoking because they were unhappy, I invariably discover, on closer examination, that the act of smoking was something they hoped would make them happy. In fact, most admit to finding some pleasure in smoking, some release from social expectations or discomforts.

I'm confident that if you examine your smoking history, you'll discover that you started smoking not because you thought it would make you unhappy, but because you were following your happiest thoughts at the moment. You were on an adventure.

My Brother's Happy Example

I was happy to start smoking when I was seven years old, at the invitation of my nine-year-old brother. He took me into our small suburban bathroom and pulled out of his sleeve, like the magician he was, one of our mother's cigarettes, which he had snitched from her pack. Since he was the veteran, he showed me how to do it. I followed his example. It tasted sweet and wondrous. We laughed and giggled, happy to think of ourselves as grown-ups.

He didn't really show me anything new, of course. I had seen my mother and her friends smoke, as well as a whole generation of World War II smokers. What my brother showed me, instead, was how to be bold, adventurous—how to be a "free thinker." Such an example, such demonstration, for me, was innocent, healthy, and life-enhancing.

Childhood is full of wonder. Although my older brother and I had several happy occasions to "sneak" a cigarette or two over the next several years, and although I, in turn, showed my younger brother how to smoke, we boys were just as happy to play football or catch frogs or ride our bikes as we were to smoke.

When I was twelve (in the sixth grade), my buddy Les Gifford and I started carrying our own smokes, because we were happy to start thinking of ourselves as "tough guys." We sought independence, maturity, new life, and smoking cigarettes seemed to fit this image perfectly. How grown-up we felt, as we slouched down the alleyways, puffing on our forbidden smokes! I realize now that it was not the cigarettes, but the *thought* of ourselves smoking the cigarettes—the adventure, the happy new way of thinking about the place we occupied in the world—that kept us puffing (and coughing!). I enjoyed the thought of "needing" a cigarette after a hard day in sixth grade. I loved how smoking cigarettes, even *needing* a cigarette, made me a real part of a wider world.

A year or so later, however, I found a new image for myself: I wanted to be a professional football player, or maybe a professional basketball player. I loved sports and was very happy to think of myself as a great athlete and no longer a tough guy or "hood." For me, at that point in my life, there was no "*giving up* smoking." I just followed my happiest thinking and the smoking fell away easily, immediately, spontaneously. I had not yet educated myself—or allowed myself to be educated—into thinking all the things I *didn't* enjoy when thinking about cigarettes. I just went on to the next thing I enjoyed, as do most kids who "try" smoking for a while and then move on.

So, for a couple of years, I was a budding world-class athlete, at least in my own mind. By early high school, it became apparent that my potential as a professional athlete was limited—I was sixty pounds lighter and six inches shorter than the rest of my team. Again, I moved on. I returned to puffing, mimicking my friends and other neighborhood heroes. Soon, I acquired the adolescent/adult smoking behaviors that would carry me through two decades.

"Love Made Me Do It"

It seems clear that we are all introduced to smoking, formally or informally, by our loved ones—our mothers and fathers or brothers or sisters or best friends down the street. My story is really no different. We started smoking because we loved the people around us—our friends and family—and we wanted to be like them. There is no need to condemn ourselves, or them, for that. We all followed our joy into this smoking behavior.

However, for those of us whose memories seem painful or foolish, we can—we must—soften those thoughts about how we started smoking. Let us honor the impulse that sought new life, new love, new ways of being in the world.

As you learn to allow yourself to follow what you most enjoy thinking, you will again find new ways of being in the world, new and wider expressions of your potential. This process can (and will!) be just as much fun as your early puffing experience. Only when you forgive yourself—when you are happy with yourself—for starting smoking, will you be truly free to move forward, ending your smoking easily, spontaneously.

Whenever thoughts or memories arise concerning your initial start of smoking, engage in the Enlightenment Exercise, and verify, "Is this what I enjoy thinking, yes or no?" By doing so, your past will begin to change for the better. And, best of all, you will become a freer, happier human being. Isn't that what it's all about?

═══════

Exercise

"Pretend" to Forget to Smoke

In the same way that you first pretended to be a smoker—even though you weren't one—you can now pretend to be a nonsmoker. You don't have to go through with it, if you don't enjoy it. Just pretend, for a minute or an hour or a day, that you're a nonsmoker. See what it feels like. See if you enjoy the new identity.

In the same way that you "tried" smoking, without making a huge commitment, you can "try" nonsmoking without making a huge commitment. But here's the rub: When you first experimented with smoking, pretending you were a smoker, you *enjoyed* trying it, even if your body set off its version of car alarms. In fact, in a strange way, you enjoyed the alarms going off. You enjoyed the coughing, the dizziness, the upset stomach. So when you try nonsmoking, see if you can capture that old, almost naughty spirit of adventure. For right now, pretend that the only reason you are trying out nonsmoking is because *you enjoy trying it*.

INSIGHT *Step-by-step, by patient, persistent effort, you can accustom yourself to nonsmoking, just as, step-by-step, through patient, persistent effort, you accustomed yourself to smoking!*

As you have probably realized by now, what we are suggesting is contrary to almost every other stop-smoking approach. Let's be contrary! Isn't it liberating, almost naughty, to realize that you don't need to make a strong commitment to becoming a nonsmoker? Not yet, anyway. (And not ever if you don't want!)

Later in the book we'll show you how you might be able to easily make a commitment to not smoking, when the time is right for you. But for now, you're a greenhorn at this stop-smoking game, and just as when you first started smoking you weren't asked to start smoking a pack a day, you now aren't being asked to give up smoking forever. Just play with it. Play at being a non-smoker for however long you feel like playing, and then don't play it any more! Move on (or back) just like you did when you started smoking. View it as an adventure, a naughty little escapade that nobody else needs to know about. Isn't that fun?

Who said stopping smoking shouldn't be fun?

"But," you say, "I've tried to quit and it *wasn't* fun"—and you still don't see how it possibly could be? In the next chapter we take a look at what probably happened as you attempted to quit in the past, and why it *will* be different this time.

8 When the Smoker Is Ready, the Smoke Disappears

Why You Haven't Quit Before, and Why You Can Quit This Time!

> For every thing, there is a season, and a time to every purpose under heaven.
> —Ecclesiastes 3.1

On the first night of an old-time stop-smoking program, sponsored by a major religious organization, and within the first ten minutes, the instructor walks around the room, holding open a brown paper bag into which everyone is ordered to deposit their cigarettes. In the process of collecting the smokes, the instructor venomously denounces tobacco and the tobacco habit and assures his audience that he never has and never will take up such a filthy practice. In teaching smokers to quit smoking, the first thing such a program does is deprive participants of cigarettes.

The reasoning behind this immediate-deprivation (*decapitation*) strategy, let's assume, is that if a smoker is motivated enough to show up for the stop-smoking class, then the time to quit is obviously right. The smoker just needs a little shove (or a big push!) to break the habit.

Although every stop-smoking method has its adherents, and every method invariably attracts individuals who want to walk down such a path and who therefore may be benefited by it, the long-term success rate of the strategy previously described, as with most other programs, is modest at best. In fact, when we consult any of the major studies of quitting rates published in the last twenty years, we find that eight or nine out of every ten people who attend such classes do *not* receive the result they were seeking.

Milder variations of this approach are more common. The first step of almost every program—whether sponsored by the American Cancer Society, the American Lung Association, the public schools or various health agencies—is education. Smokers are educated, overtly or covertly, about how terrible tobacco is. This strategy ("Tobacco is terrible! Get rid of it now!") may account for the dismal success rates of most stop-smoking programs. Here's why.

Quitting in this way is like having an amputation. And people don't *want* amputations. Their inner voice assures them that they can be whole. That they *are* whole! People, knowingly or not, want a complete healing of their smoking unhappiness and thus are quite reluctant to settle for an amputation.

Where You Were

When you first started smoking, as we discussed in Chapter 7, you wanted to experience something new, exciting, adventurous in yourself and in the world around you. You were hungry for life. Tobacco, in some respects, delivered that expanded life experience.

When you continued with your smoking, wasn't it because you wanted to explore more deeply this new world, this new identity you had discovered? Through smoking, you were able to experience some semblance of adulthood: the tangible reality of your expanding identity and the pleasures such an identity provided. When you took up smoking you wanted a taste of personal freedom and pleasure. And smoking did indeed give you that feeling of freedom and pleasure.

So when you are told how horrible tobacco is, how bad it is for your health and life, and how nothing good can come of using it, you only half-believe. You might accept such findings intellectually, but there's something deeper in you, connected with your whole life history, that knows that such assertions tell only part of the story.

But you probably started smoking a long time ago and have by now pretty much learned the lessons of smoking. The adventure has been lived, and now you likely sense that you're ready for a new level, more advanced lessons, a higher adventure.

Before we move on, let's reiterate what we've learned in previous chapters: The reason you haven't quit smoking—for good, that is—is because you didn't enjoy quitting. You already knew, at one level or another, that joy is the most important thing for you and for all of those around you. Quitting *without joy* would be like having something amputated. That isn't the type of healing any of us desires. We want to be *whole!*

When people do stop smoking suddenly, without finishing the course they are taking, some try to replace their smoking habits with other physical habits in order to "fill" the hole left by the amputation. These substitute habits may last only briefly, or they may be lifelong. This phenomenon—trying to fill the space left by amputation—is one reason traditional stop-smoking programs must work so hard to help their successful students curb newfound eating habits. (We'll discuss this more in Chapter 8.) Others may pick up a lifelong "toothpick" habit, or gum chewing, or teeth grinding. Some people find that their sexual appetites increase dramatically. Others may begin working or playing cards excessively.

Many believe that these "substitute habits" are much less harmful than the tobacco habit, and from a strictly physical point of view this is generally the case. But you are not reading this book simply to prolong the life of your physical body. If, by quitting smoking without joy, you deprive yourself of emotional, mental, and spiritual growth, you pay a hefty price for your success.

From an enlightened perspective, it was your inner wisdom that prevented you from stopping smoking before reading this book. Sure, you could have quit in another way, but you didn't, so you might as well assume that you were seeking a higher, truer path!

If you're still smoking, let that be sufficient evidence that before now you simply weren't ready to quit. Before this moment, the time wasn't right for you to quit for good, so you didn't and that was wise. You knew, at least from a subconscious level, what was good for you and what wasn't. You didn't want amputation. You had something more to learn, something more to understand about this whole smoking process. You weren't ready to quit yet, and so you didn't. Good for you! No blame is necessary.

As Lao Tzu wrote, "When the student is ready, the teacher appears." Is there anyone who has not experienced the truth of this maxim, to a greater or lesser extent, in his or her own life education?

Where You Are

Let's assume that you are now ready to stop smoking, and that your own happiness has appeared in the form of this book to teach you the next step in the journey. (You are free to choose this assumption!)

Many enlightened teachings suggest that your individual purpose here on Earth, in one way or another, is to help elevate the consciousness of all mankind. You are here to help cleanse humanity's collective past and to prepare the way for a higher, brighter collective future. You do this through love and joy.

The reason this is your job, your purpose here on Earth, is because, in fact, at root each of us is one with the collective humanity. You are an individual expression of the whole.

According to a wide variety of enlightenment teachings, the way you elevate world consciousness is first by taking on flesh in the world (that is, being born into the world), which means that you also take on, to a certain extent, all of the problems, hang-ups, diseases, and pollutants to which flesh is heir. This "taking on" process occurs not only at the time of your birth, but throughout your childhood, adolescence, and young adulthood, as you are educated by your parents, teachers, friends, and culture to the ways of the world.

Once you have taken on flesh and the forms and features of your time and place, then, the enlightenment teachings tell us, it is your job to transform and elevate these conditions into a higher expression. In this way, then, by cleansing and purifying your life, you potentially cleanse and purify the world.

An extreme example of this "taking on" was related by Baba Ram Dass during his early public tours. He told of meeting an Indian "smoking yogi," who spent many years taking on the karma of smokers and junk-food addicts. The yogi sat, without moving, in the same place for many years. (Observers watched to see if he would get up to go to the restroom or eat—he didn't!) The "smoking yogi" smoked ten cigarettes—five in each hand—at one time; the cigarettes were given to him by people who wanted to quit. He also drank gallons of Pepsi and Coca Cola. These were his only ingestants. His work, he said, was to help purify the world of these addictions, by transmuting their energies in his own body.

To a certain extent, every smoker functions as a "smoking yogi," by taking on the karma of the whole smoking world and transmuting it in his or her own body. For most smokers, however, this is not a conscious process, and thus not very efficient or speedy.

At a very mundane level, when a smoker quits smoking, he or she helps purify the world by being an example for and an inspiration to other smokers who want to quit. On the other hand, quitting also eliminates the potential that one person has to model harmful smoking behaviors for other people. (It has been shown that children of smokers are more likely to pick up the habit than children of nonsmokers.)

Where You Are Going

At a more subtle level, however, the inner processes of liberation you go through as you find your personal freedom from tobacco help, if only in a small way, all people, present and future. As you elevate your consciousness, find your joy, you open the door for others. When you accept happiness into your life and consciousness as a daily presence, it spreads. In this way, you help others find freedom from tobacco and freedom from whatever their problem or addiction might be. Happiness heals!

When we set to rest our struggles with tobacco and find peace (joy!), the effect reverberates to others, both near and far. And the peace that you realize and share after such a long struggle can be much more effective, much deeper and more healing than if you had not entered the struggle at all.

Of course, you are perfectly free to doubt these subtle enlightened approaches. What you don't want to doubt, however, is whether you are enjoying yourself today, this hour, this moment. If you doubt everything else in the world, but have no doubt that you are enjoying yourself, by enjoying all of your thoughts, then your freedom, your liberation is assured, and the world *will* benefit from your happy certainty!

If you still feel hesitant or resistant about engaging in the Enlightenment Exercise—that is, thinking what you most enjoy thinking—begin by enjoying your hesitancy, enjoying your resistance. As you enjoy your hesitancy, your resistance, you will discover at once that joy is the empowering presence in your life, as it is in all of our lives.

Smoking has been your teacher for many years. In the present context, a natural extension of Lao Tzu's adage, "When the student is ready, the teacher appears," is, "When the student is ready, the teacher [smoking] disappears!" Congratulations! You've learned what you needed to learn from that teacher, and it's time to move on. Thankfully, when a door closes, a window opens.

Exercise

1. When you next see a young person smoking, rather than indulge an automatic, negative judgment, silently recall what

you were like at that age and simply *enjoy* the adolescent foolishness you observe. Withholding negative judgment will help both you and the young person to find freedom from such foolishness more quickly.

2. When you see other adults smoking, imagine them as young people who are just beginning their experiments with smoking. Again, enjoy them for it. As you generate such silent, compassionate feelings toward other smokers, you are helping them and yourself become free of the addiction.

In the next chapter, we look at a set of chains that bind you to the smoking room, and we discuss the key that unlocks such chains. Keep reading!

9 The Path of Forgiveness

How to Heal Your Past, Your Present, and Your Future (And Probably Your Lungs, while You're at It!)

> Happiness is serious. Very serious.
> —Hugh Prather

In *Chicken Soup for the Soul*, Jack Canfield and Mark Hansen tell the story of a young couple who had a second child after their daughter reached the age of five. The daughter appeared thrilled with the new baby but kept asking her parents if she might be left alone with the infant. Having heard stories of sibling jealousy and the innocent desire to have things return to what they were before the baby was born, the parents were reluctant to grant the little girl's wish for time alone with the new baby. But the little girl persisted in her request. Finally, the parents installed a remote listening device in the infant's crib, and then granted their daughter's request for a private visit with the baby. After the parents left the baby's room, the little girl leaned down to the baby and whispered, "Tell me again what heaven is like. I'm starting to forget."

At heart, we are all spiritual beings "sent from heaven." The fundamental nature of the very consciousness with which you are reading this book is infinite, eternal, joyous. Sometimes, of course, if you're like the rest of us, you forget or ignore this fact.

When we forget that we are spiritual beings, we are then

compelled to seek happiness, satisfaction, and our daily sustenance from the people, places, and things in the world around us. When we forget we are spiritual beings, we assume we are on our own, separate, and apart.

Conversely, when we remember we are spiritual beings, when we remember the happiness that is the nature of our consciousness, then we spontaneously pour forth this happiness into the world around us. We discover that this happiness has within it all forms and thus that all we need comes to us from within. We are no longer compelled to spend our days grasping and clawing for some kind of sustenance. Rather, having learned to trust that which is pouring forth from within, we recognize that our every need is met.

> Seek not what ye shall eat, or what ye shall drink, neither be ye of doubtful mind .... But rather seek ye the kingdom of God, [happiness] and all these things shall be added onto you.
> —(Luke 12: 29, 31)

INSIGHT *When we remember who we are and what we are, we know that we are here* for giving. *When we ignore or deny this native state of being, we then see ourselves as here* for getting. *Practicing the Enlightenment Exercise, we remember ourselves with the wider reality, the joyous universe.*

The practice of forgiving, in its truest sense, is the act of giving our joy. When we forgive, we look with joy and compassion at those people who seem to have "trespassed against us." That is, we freely give our innate happiness, our innate joy to the people who would not, from surface appearances, necessarily deserve such a gift.

How We Forgive

We forgive someone by changing our thoughts about them and about their deeds. This change of thought is a gift we share with them. In effect, we change our thoughts from those that we do not enjoy to those that we do enjoy. We give these more enjoyable thoughts either silently or aloud, in person or from a distance. As long as we continue to hold thoughts that we do not enjoy, we have not forgiven.

This type of giving can be deeply healing, not just for recently committed wrongs against us, but for anything that has happened to us in our lifetimes. Dr. Raymond Moody, in *True Tales of Reincarnation*, suggests that we also must forgive and thus heal people and resolve events that happened to us in previous lives.

Leonard Orr, author of *Rebirthing in the Modern Age*, has demonstrated in thousands of cases that it is possible to heal and forgive even those offenses which were committed against us in the womb. He has documented the healing efficacy of remembering our own births and prenatal experiences.

Orr recounts how he explored his own prebirth memories and discovered that his mother had been very upset when she found out she was pregnant. She did not want to have this child. Orr says he was willing to comply with his mother's wishes and worked to hang himself while still in the womb, by coiling the umbilical cord around his neck. He was in fact a "blue baby" when born.

With maturity, and a more enlightened perspective, Orr at last recognized the fear and worry his mother experienced, the same fear and worry every mother experiences to a certain extent. He no longer resented his mother's attitudes at birth or during his childhood troubles. He changed his thoughts, and by doing so, he was healed of disorders that he had had since birth. The rebirthing movement that Orr founded has documented thousands of physical healings—from deafness to paralysis to asthma—that have resulted from the process of "forgiving" the trauma surrounding the birth event itself as well as problems during the first twenty-four months of life.

Still, the difficulties we need to resolve (forgive!) are generally more contemporary and do not necessarily arise from such long-standing relationships or ills. Louise Hay, author of *Heal Your Life* and numerous other inspirational best-selling books and tapes, recounts how, when she was diagnosed with cancer, she determined to make a complete recovery by removing from her mind all of the thoughts and attitudes that she habitually held and that clearly were "eating at her." This joyful inner surgery, which was accompanied by a spontaneous change of lifestyle including relocation to a different state and changing occupation, did indeed bring Hay back to a natural state of wholeness and health. Her experiences with forgiving herself and those around her have led thousands of others down similar healing paths. She teaches people how to heal the "lumps of resentment" and the "sores" of irritation. Physical and mental healing accompany this complete return to joy.

Such forgiveness and healing improves more than our own physical and mental well-being. A recent report of a young woman who was studying Christian Science demonstrates how one's inner happiness is the most important thing for everybody.

This young woman had not heard from her father, who had a history of alcoholism, in more than five years. During one week in particular, the woman worked hard to understand that her true father was her Father in heaven and that every human being is a spiritual being, regardless of what physical appearances might suggest. On a particular Sunday afternoon, the woman realized at a very deep level that her patrimony was spiritual, joyous, and perfect. On this day, she was able to release all of the pent-up antagonism, bitterness, and resentment she harbored against her earthly father, realizing that he and every other person is, at root, spiritual, free, and whole. Recognizing the omnipotence of the heavenly Father, she experienced a deep, healing peace in her thoughts about her relationship with her earthly father.

Several weeks later, for the first time in five years, her father contacted her. He told her that two weeks previously, on Sunday afternoon, he had been resting on the bank of a river, bottle at his side, destitute and apparently hopeless. Suddenly, he realized he no longer had the desire to drink. He no longer was satisfied with the life he had been living. He stood up, walked away, and was now returning to a useful, dignified, and much happier life. His desire to drink had vanished completely.

This story demonstrates how the enlightened, joyful work we do in our own consciousness inevitably has a powerful and far-reaching influence, not only on those we know but around the world.

The same healing action occurs when we recognize that we are here for giving happiness, even after the most traumatic, violent, and horrific of experiences. For example, many support groups have been formed by people who have gone through such nightmares as the murder of a child, the suicide of a loved one, rape or incest, or the diagnosis of aids* or other purportedly incurable ailments. (There's no such thing as "incurable," says Louise Hay. Absolutely every "incurable" ailment has been cured by someone, at some time, which demonstrates that *no* ailment is absolutely incurable!)

Less traumatic, but equally disturbing experiences have also spurred support groups around the world. Everything from the loss of a beloved pet, to the loss of a job, to the loss of hair is now subject to "support group" therapy.

Although it may not be clear to those who lead such groups, the basic cure for the unhappiness initially expressed by members is a change in their thoughts. This "thought transformation" is what the members of support groups help each other do. Certainly, we recognize the depth and intensity of the situations that caused the unhappiness, and are not flippantly suggesting, "Just don't think about it," or "Just get over it." Rather, we are suggesting that no matter what the outer experience, the inner spirit, the inner happiness remains intact, inviolate, ready to be brought forth again in its proper season. Such work may take time, or it may happen quite quickly. But wholeness, depth, and maturity of spirit are possible for every person, no matter what the experiences of this life, be they recent or in the distant past, personal or familial.

---

* In keeping with the practice suggested by Louise Hay and adopted by many people who work with people with aids, we do not capitalize the word *aids*.

So what does all of this have to do with smoking? There's a tendency in our culture to heap huge amounts of abuse on ourselves for smoking. And if we don't do it to ourselves—which would be rare—then the people around us are happy to take up the chore!

You forgive yourself for smoking simply because it is the healthiest thing you can do, for yourself and for all those around you. Most smokers have ten, twenty, thirty, or more years of smoking history. If your thoughts are not in harmony with all those years, then your thoughts are not in harmony with your life.

You do not need to stop smoking before you forgive yourself for smoking. In fact, such forgiveness is itself a very liberating act, a precious gift you can give yourself. If you continue to beat yourself up, condemn yourself, and hold unpleasant images of yourself, you shackle yourself, you weigh yourself down. Such activities deplete the energy you could otherwise use for attaining and sustaining a higher (more joyful!) state of mind.

So, how do you do it, how do you forgive yourself for smoking? You already know....

The Enlightenment Exercise

1. *The Law of Happiness*. Enjoying my happiness is the most important thing for me and for everybody around me.
2. *The Law of Linkage*. I enjoy my happiness when I enjoy the thought I am thinking in this moment.
3. *The Law of Spontaneity*. Whenever necessary, I ask myself, *Am I enjoying this thought [or this line of thought]—yes or no?* If the answer is not an immediate and spontaneous *"yes,"* then it's a *"no."*

4. *The Law of Joyous Action.* If I discover I am not enjoying my thoughts right now, then I am not free. I then have two options:

- I can choose to drop the thought [or the line of thought] that I do not enjoy, and choose instead a thought [or a line of thought] that I enjoy more; or
- I can choose to enjoy the thought [or the line of thought] that a moment before I was not enjoying—either as it is, or by changing its form, size, texture, position, place, or voice.

To forgive yourself, or anybody else, you simply engage in the Enlightenment Exercise. There is no other way to truly forgive! Just saying, "I forgive you," to yourself or somebody else may be a start toward forgiveness, but it doesn't really get the job done. You must drop the thoughts you don't enjoy and begin thinking thoughts you do enjoy. That's true forgiveness. (This shouldn't be a hard case to win. After all, do you want to eat dirt pie with worms or blueberry pie with whipped cream?)

When you begin "relieving" your past and all those in it, by reliving it with thoughts you enjoy, here, now, you discover that the harm you did to yourself and others is likewise beginning to be relieved. When you enjoy your thoughts, your lungs find rest. When you enjoy your thoughts, your heart finds rhythm. When you enjoy your thoughts, your arteries expand.

This is not just wishful thinking. Scientific research on the beneficial physiological effects of good mental health is vast and indisputable. By healing your thoughts and feelings—by enjoying your thoughts and feelings—you heal your physical body as well.

So when should you start? With your next thought. And then the next one. And the one after that. For the rest of your (eternal and infinite) life.

———

Exercises

When I ask, "Who are you most angry at, right now?" who first comes to mind?

How could you change your thoughts about that person so you could enjoy your thoughts more? (Note that I didn't ask how you could change that person, but how you could change your *thoughts* about that person.) Would you make your thoughts smaller? Dimmer? Further away? You don't necessarily have to completely, totally enjoy your thoughts about that person to begin with. You need only do something with your thoughts to allow you to enjoy your thoughts a *little more* than you do now. Step by step, you move out of the morass.

(Radical hint: You don't necessarily have to make your thoughts of the other person positive! Joy is the key. You might enjoy thinking of that person with a lamp shade on his or her head, or dressed in bloomers, or on his or her knees apologizing—anything to restore your own sense of joy!)

Okay, who are the next three people you are angry or upset with? One at a time, work with your thoughts of those people until you enjoy them.

Now, what institutions are you angry at?

What groups?

If you haven't consciously done this type of "inner cleansing" work before, don't feel you have to get the whole basement/garage cleaned at once. You might need a week or two (or more) to cleanse your entire system of all resentment, all antagonism and bitterness. But, believe me, you will feel healing benefits from even one session!

You can always determine the best people, groups, and institutions to "work on"—to cleanse your thoughts and feelings about—simply by paying attention to your thoughts. The ones to work on are the ones that are coming up right now!

We've come a long way. In the next chapter, we'll look at practical things you can do in the days and weeks before quitting.

10 On Your Mark, Get Set, Get Set . . .

Getting Ready to Quit

> The longest journey begins with a single step.
> —Chinese proverb

In the old way of looking at your smoking you generally had only two views: smoking and not smoking. You are already very familiar with this conflict. When you are smoking, you often wish that you were not smoking. And when you are not smoking, you often wish that you were.

Most smokers, at one point or another in their lives, try to give up smoking. When they do, they often discover that the harder they try—the more they tell themselves, "I shouldn't, I shouldn't, I shouldn't"—the quicker they say, *"Okay, okay, okay"* and continue to smoke.

There's a saying frequently encountered in the enlightenment literature: "What you resist, persists." This mirrors Newton's Third Law: For every action, there's an equal and opposite reaction. Mark Twain also said it well: "As Christian children, we learned at an early age the joys of the forbidden fruit." What is forbidden is immediately attractive.

In the enlightened approach to smoking, we add a third element to the battle of opposites, of should versus shouldn't. We bring in joy. And when we do that, we find the battle immediately begins to wane. By introducing joy, the question is no longer whether you are or are not smoking, but rather whether you are consciously *enjoying* yourself no matter what you are doing!

We've covered enough material that by now some readers are probably thinking, "Okay, okay, enough already. We're ready to give it a shot. We're ready to be happy to quit. But how and when should we do it? Right now? Next week? Next month? Let's get on with it! What do we do, exactly? Should we set a quit date? How do we start to stop?"

Other readers, of course, are happy just to continue with Step One—just reading, hanging out—though they'd probably be willing to watch as the brave ones jump in. (See Chapter 1 for the Seven Steps to Quitting.)

As you'll learn in the next few chapters, choosing the proper time and place to quit—the proper "quit date"—is not nearly as important as preparing properly for such a quit date, which really is the focus of this book. Though you might find the perfect time, the perfect place, with all outer conditions seeming exactly right, if you haven't prepared properly within, the quit date simply won't work.

On the other hand, once you have your "inner work" done and the groundwork laid, you may discover that you don't even need a quit date, because your quitting has already happened, or because it's already happening, or because you're inspired to do it in the middle of a Monday morning rush hour. When the inner work is done, the right time and right place will be obvious to you.

So what does this inner work entail? First, of course, is the Enlightenment Exercise. Not only is it helpful to have recognized the value of the Law of Happiness in theory, but you must be brave enough to begin living your life guided by your inner joy. That's the radical approach here outlined.

This means managing your thinking not with what you believe to be true, or what others say is true, or in accordance with what you *should* be thinking, but rather in accordance with what you *enjoy* thinking. Choose thoughts you enjoy. Drop thoughts you don't enjoy. Choose to enjoy thoughts you did not enjoy in the past. Change (play with!) your thoughts—making them larger, smaller, brighter, dimmer, closer, farther away—to make them more enjoyable. Do this not just occasionally but habitually, as a chosen way of thinking about yourself and the world. Simply beginning this process may be enough to move you gracefully, effortlessly into freedom from tobacco.

Obey the Basic Law

Your strategy for quitting and getting ready to quit is simply to enjoy yourself "one thought at a time"—an approach similar to the "one day at a time" strategy of Alcoholics Anonymous.

Whenever necessary, ask yourself, "Am I enjoying this thought [or this line of thought], yes or no?" If the answer is not an immediate and spontaneous "yes," it's a "no."

If you're not enjoying yourself, that is, if you're not enjoying the thought you are thinking, you can return to joy by simply following the Law of Joyous Action, which gives you two options: Either

1. *Drop the thought you do not enjoy and think something you do enjoy instead*; or
2. *Enjoy the thought that you did not enjoy a moment before.*

That's the simple enlightenment process, the Enlightenment Exercise. It's a strategy that actually works, quickly and easily, to free you from your smoking habit. But for the process to work, you must use it!

Is this strategy different from traditional stop-smoking strategies? Yes, in some basic ways, this strategy is completely different, it has a completely different foundation. In practice, however, it can work the same way. In fact, combining a few traditional strategies with this enlightened approach gives you a chance to double your happy quitting power.

The Traditional Path

In the stop-smoking literature, there's a delightful little book called *Quit,* by Charles F. Wetherall. This little book is printed in the size and shape of a cigarette pack, and there are now over one million copies in print. It's one of the classics, and it clearly articulates the traditional stop-smoking approach. Without doubt, many smokers have used this little book to help them quit. We'll use it for this, too, but in a different way. Basically, Wetherall offers a five-step system for quitting:

1. Determine why you want to quit smoking.
2. Rank your cigarettes for their importance to your lifestyle on a scale of 1 to 3—3 being the most important and 1 being a cigarette you smoke unconsciously.
3. Gradually reduce your cigarette smoking.
4. Quit.
5. Guard against resumption of smoking.

You probably are familiar with the general thrust of this traditional strategy; it is one many professionals suggest. When you play the

Enlightenment Game with this little book—to ensure that you *enjoy* Wetherall's strategy—you discover empowering insights and practical suggestions for mastering the smoking process.

First, "Determine why you want to quit smoking." Most stop-smoking programs ask you to do a variation of this same step, because most assume that if you can just come up with enough "good reasons," then the good reasons can empower you to quit.

You probably already have a handful of good reasons to quit. And if you can't come up with enough good reasons by yourself, then your doctor, your spouse, your children, your co-workers, and even strangers will be happy to supply you with so many good reasons that you'll have good reasons falling out of all your pockets! Good reasons for quitting smoking are not rare in this world.

From an enlightened perspective, however, you really only need one tiny, insignificant, no-account reason to quit smoking as long as that one reason is a reason that you truly enjoy! This enjoyable reason for quitting doesn't have to be logical, noble, respectable, or high-minded. It can be half-baked, illogical, off-the-wall, and nonsensical, as long as you really enjoy thinking about it.

If you secretly enjoy your reason for quitting—if it makes you smile inside—then that goofy little reason will be more than reason enough to quit. You don't just need reasons to help you quit smoking—you need reasons that you feel, that tickle you, that ignite your enjoyable thoughts. If you have just one such thought, even a tiny little sliver of a reason that excites your pleasurable thoughts, then that little sliver of joy will give you the full power to do what you want.

Here's why: When your "quit day" has come and you're not smoking anymore, you may have moments when your thoughts start racing, searching for good reasons to start again. You'll probably think about abandoning your decision to quit. You'll think about just giving up this stop-smoking nonsense. It's in these moments of doubt that your little pleasure, your secret joy returns to you and dissolves those other thoughts. If you have joy, even though it is as small in size as a mustard seed, it will move the mountain of your smoking habit. Just a little joy will do it.

The truth of the matter is that everybody who has ever quit successfully has done so because of a reason they enjoyed. They, or their teachers, may not have been conscious that an enjoyable reason gave them the power to quit, but if you look close enough you'll discover it did.

On the other hand, if you have five hundred good reasons for quitting—all of which may be scientifically sound, intellectually adept, and politically correct, but none of which you personally especially enjoy—then you still won't have enough good reasons to quit, or enough will power, or stick-to-it-ness. Your joy is what gives you the power to succeed.

Here's the good news and why the Enlightenment Exercise is so useful: You can *choose* to enjoy any reason you select. Through the processes already outlined, you can invest the time and energy necessary to discover and embrace your delight in this area of your life. You can *choose* to enjoy yourself and your reasons more. Do you see now why the enlightenment process is so effective?

═══

Exercise

Enlightened Preparation for Quit Day

1. In your smoking journal, list ten things you personally will enjoy about quitting.

2. Now list ten things you personally enjoy already about *not* quitting!

By writing out these reasons—for quitting and for *not* quitting—you are taking the traditional approach one step further and setting yourself on the path to success immediately, whether you are smoking or not. This exercise will help you to be aware of exactly where and how you will be enjoying yourself in the weeks ahead, as your quit date approaches and your smoking habit is consciously dissolved from your life.

In this exercise you may find it useful to list some of the "traditional" reasons for quitting—those reasons that come up when you first think about it. For instance, let's say your first ten good reasons for quitting are:

1. When I stop smoking, I'll stop beating myself up all the time.
2. When I stop smoking, my overall physical health will be better.
3. I'll save money.
4. When I stop smoking, my mouth and breath will feel fresher.
5. My lungs will feel cleaner.
6. My family will admire me more.
7. My co-workers will admire me more.
8. When I stop smoking, I'll have more "breath" to walk and run and move about with.
9. As a nonsmoker, my clothes will be fresher.
10. When I stop smoking, I'll have a higher opinion of myself.

Here's more good news: By engaging in the Enlightenment Exercise, *you don't have to wait until you quit smoking before you start enjoying your happiness* in the exact same ways that you have outlined!

The Joys of Quitting (or Not)

For example, as you practice the Enlightenment Exercise, you naturally, spontaneously stop beating yourself up (item 1). You don't have to stop smoking to stop beating yourself up!

And as you enjoy each thought, each feeling, then your overall physical health (item 2) also improves, *whether you smoke or not*. As Deepak Chopra points out, "Joy is both the prophylactic and curative healing agent." You don't have to wait until you stop smoking to enjoy better physical health. As you experience your usual amount of joy, every day, the result is that your physical health—your circulation, your breathing, your digestion—begins to improve, immediately!

As you practice the enlightenment process, you naturally begin saving money (item 3) because you discover that your joy is already intact and it's free. By enjoying yourself naturally, you are not as often tempted to try to "buy" happiness. Your wants gradually diminish. Your pleasures simplify. You find yourself paying more attention to what you already have, and you are not so concerned with what you don't have. Your possessions last longer. You're not always in such a hurry to exchange your money for whatever promises to heal your sorrow. Your sorrow diminishes.

Let's continue.

Whether you smoke or not, when you practice the Enlightenment Exercise your mouth and breath are fresher (item 4), first figuratively, because your words are sweeter, softer, kinder. And second, more directly, because when you play the Enlightenment Game you're more alert, more willing to take time to remain "refreshed" throughout the day. You find it easy, natural, to do what you need to do, when you need to do it, simply because you *enjoy* it.

Playing the Enlightenment Game you also appreciate your lungs (item 5) and your breathing much more than you have. To simply enjoy your breathing, the process of inhaling and exhaling—smoke-filled or not—is one of the first, most basic ways to enjoy your happiness. You don't need to quit smoking before you enjoy your breathing and your lungs more consciously.

INSIGHT *Enjoy happiness now!*

I'm sure you can see what we're doing here. When you make your list of reasons for quitting smoking, you map out for yourself more enjoyable roads down which you want to travel. With the enlightenment process you can begin traveling down those roads—indeed, enjoying the benefits—now.

Practicing your joy—playing this Enlightenment Game in your thoughts and in your journal-writing—fills up your tank with happiness. Many smokers head off on the long journey of quitting with an empty tank of happiness. They falsely assume that if they just quit smoking, that will bring them all the happiness they need. This is not the case. It's no wonder these folks don't reach their destination! The "quitting journey" is fueled by happiness. It's best to start with a full tank!

Start enjoying your freedom from the first day! We encourage you (again and again!) to start filling up your tank with happiness, by using the Enlightenment Exercise regularly. Once your tank is full, you'll be able to travel to all sorts of wonderful new places. There will be no stopping you!

So what was our next traditional reason for quitting? Ahh, yes—for your family's sake and for the sake of your co-workers (items 6 and 7, respectively).

This will be no surprise. You do not need to quit smoking before you start enjoying your family and your co-workers. As you enjoy yourself more and allow your own native happiness to come out more and more, your family and your co-workers will quickly pick up the cue. You will enjoy each other more, whether you are smoking or not, when you enjoy the thoughts and feelings you are experiencing right now.

The next reason for quitting was so you would be able to run better, walk better, move around with more breath (item 8). You'll discover that accessing your natural happiness creates energy. Everyone who practices this exercise reports this delightful effect. As you let your inner joy fill and surround your life, you'll find yourself moving with a lighter step. You'll be more willing, more able, more energized for your next adventure. As you practice the enlightenment process, you'll discover that you have more energy than ever before, and it will have nothing whatsoever to do with whether you smoke or not.

When you let more joy into your life, you start wearing only those clothes you're happy to wear (item 9). And you wear them more gracefully, elegantly, appropriately. Practicing your happiness is the best thing that could happen to your wardrobe!

When you practice the Enlightenment Exercise, you immediately have a higher opinion of yourself (item 10). And you also have a higher opinion of the people around you and of the world you live in, whether you smoke or not.

So these examples are obvious, yes? The point is that *all of the traditional reasons that you or anybody else might offer for quitting are based on your happiness*. So begin enjoying yourself more without delay, *right now!* The smoking will then take care of itself. And when you do stop smoking, of course, the joy you started experiencing today will simply deepen, broaden, intensify.

The Joys of Smoking (or Not)

Now let's go a little bit further—let's get *radically* happy! What are ten good (i.e., enjoyable) and/or traditional reasons to continue smoking? How about:

1. When I smoke, the coffee seems to taste better.
2. Smoking soothes my nerves.
3. Smoking helps me concentrate.
4. Smoking gives me a break, helps me relax.
5. Smoking helps me digest after a good meal.
6. Smoking is a social "ice-breaker."
7. It's a social defense mechanism.
8. Smoking tastes good.
9. Smoking feels so physical, so good, in my lungs.
10. Smoking makes sex more "complete."

A review of these reasons for continuing to smoke from the perspective of what we've already learned about the enlightenment process will be quite revealing. Are you ready?

Most often, with your first cup of coffee and your first smoke (item 1), you give yourself permission to enjoy, to relax, to think what you are happiest thinking for a minute or two before the day starts. The Enlightenment Exercise gives you such permission *all* the time, whether you're smoking or not. What makes the coffee taste better is enjoying your thoughts and feelings while you drink it, *not* whether you smoke.

And as far as soothing your nerves (item 2), not enjoying your thoughts is the real nerve-racker. Enjoying your thoughts and feelings is a "nerve soother," nerve refresher. When you practice enjoying your thoughts, your nerves are soothed, whether you smoke or not.

Moving on.

Thoughts you enjoy naturally remain in your consciousness longer, so when you practice the Enlightenment Exercise, your concentration is naturally enhanced (item 3). When you say smoking helps you concentrate, you're saying your smoking gives you permission to enjoy what you're doing in the moment. Practice giving yourself such permission—permission to enjoy yourself, moment by moment, regardless of whether you smoke or not.

Okay, you say smoking gives you a much-needed break (item 4). A break from what? When you drop the habit of daily hassles and instead simply enjoy your life, by consciously enjoying your thoughts and feelings—with or without a cigarette—you discover you are always taking the most relaxing break you've ever had! And it's a break that lasts!

You say smoking helps you enjoy and digest a good meal (item

5). When you choose to think thoughts you enjoy while you're eating, every meal becomes a delight, from beginning to end, regardless of what is served. And a happy frame of mind is the basis for good digestion! It is not your smoking but rather your enjoyment of your thoughts and feelings that determines your level of contentment with your food.

As far as smoking being a social "ice breaker" (item 6), everyone is naturally attracted to a happy person. Everyone is spontaneously comfortable with such a person. So when you are enjoying yourself, *you* are the ice breaker, not your cigarette. When you enjoy yourself, you spontaneously help others to enjoy themselves. Happiness is extremely contagious!

Happiness is also the truest and most powerful defense mechanism (item 7), as it consistently puts you in the right place at the right time with the right people, saying the right things. And following your happiness will spontaneously and gracefully take you away from those people and situations that may not be right for you at this time.

As you begin enjoying your thoughts and feelings more, not only your taste (item 8) but *all* of your physical senses come alive. As you more consciously enjoy your life, your senses become cleaner, clearer, more acute than they've ever been (item 9).

Your sexual relations (item 10) reveal their natural depth and beauty and delicate vibrancy as you enjoy all that you are and all that your partner is. As you more perfectly enjoy your thoughts and feelings, you more perfectly enjoy your mate (or even the absence of a mate!). Your level of sexual joy is enhanced tenfold when you honor the presence of your own and your partner's native happiness, not only in your physical sexual encounters but in the "daily encounters" that act as spontaneously extended foreplay. (Even doing the dishes together can be a very erotic and satisfying encounter!)

Again, you see the point: Your reasons for smoking are basically so that you might enjoy yourself more. As you practice the Enlightenment Exercise in more areas of your life, the motivation for not smoking and smoking is immediately fulfilled. Thus you discover that smoking or not smoking is beside the point. Happiness is key! In this way, you move into natural, effortless mastery of the smoking process. You are free.

Exercise

If—when—you are ready to move more aggressively toward quitting, then one of the next steps might be to write out as you did for the previous exercise, ten *more* reasons you will enjoy quitting, then ten *more* reasons you enjoy smoking.

Write them out so you can appreciate them with your physical senses (e.g., by seeing them or by reading them aloud and hearing them). And then move through the reasons and see how you might find more joy in your life today, right now, using these same reasons as your guide, as demonstrated in this chapter.

By continually writing out your reasons for quitting and not quitting, using the filter of joy you will be much more clear and confident about exactly where and how the smoking habit both appears and dissolves from your life.

In the next (very brief!) chapter, we'll suggest fifty things you are free to quit right now, whether you are smoking or not smoking.

11 Fifty Other Ways to Leave Your Lover!

> Every now and then a man's mind is stretched by a new idea and never shrinks back to its original proportion.
> —Oliver Wendell Holmes

You are much closer now than ever before to being able to quit smoking successfully. Enjoy that thought! So let's do a quick rundown of some things you are free to quit now *before* you actually quit smoking. You will enjoy these same things as you quit smoking and after you quit smoking, but you might as well start enjoying them now!

You are, of course, free to change, rearrange, discard, or deny any of these items, just as you are free to consider them your "stepping stones" out of the habit. Whether you still smoke or not, you are already naturally, natively free!

1. You are free to quit trying to figure out why you can't quit!
2. You are free (right now!) to quit condemning yourself for starting to smoke in the first place.
3. You are free to quit setting a date for when you'll quit.
4. You are free to quit trying to figure out what you'll do with your hands once you have quit.
5. You are free to quit trying to figure out what you'll put in your mouth once you quit.
6. You are allowed to stop trying to cut down or cut back.
7. You are allowed to stop trying to figure out how to quit.
8. You are free to stop trying to find a perfect time to quit.

9. You are allowed to stop trying to muster up the emotional energy to quit.

10. You are allowed to stop trying to make God pay attention to your smoking habit.

11. You are free to stop trying to justify your smoking to yourself or others.

12. You are free to stop asking yourself, "Is this the moment, (the week, the month, the year) for me to quit?"

13. You are free to stop being irritated with smokers who have already quit.

14. You are free to stop worrying about whether you should smoke another one right now.

15. You are free to stop worrying about your health.

16. You are free to quit worrying about what your family says.

17. You are allowed to quit worrying about going outside at awkward times to grab a smoke.

18. You are allowed to quit feeling guilty about asking for a smoking table at restaurants.

19. You are allowed to quit worrying about whether your friends will kid you when you stop smoking.

20. You are allowed to quit worrying about the money you presently spend on smokes.

21. You are free to stop trying to find reasons as to why the enlightenment method won't work!

22. You are free to stop worrying about whether this is the right time and place for you to smoke.

23. You are free to stop trying to find a teacher to teach you how to quit.

24. You are free to stop looking for a mechanical or chemical

device that will help you to stop smoking.

25. You are free to stop believing, and stop saying, that you don't know how to quit.

26. You are allowed to quit being sarcastic about your own chances for quitting.

27. You are allowed to quit saying, thinking, and feeling that you are not yet ready to quit.

28. You are allowed to quit assuming that you personally need your tobacco more than anyone in the history of the world has ever needed tobacco.

29. You are allowed to quit feeling that you are sexy or not sexy for smoking.

30. You are free to quit saying or thinking, "I need a cigarette."

31. You are free to stop asking God what you should do about your smoking.

32. You are free to stop thinking that this secret urge to smoke makes you bad.

33. You are free to stop worrying that if you don't have a smoke right now, you'll miss out on something good.

34. You are free to stop planning your day according to how, when, and where you are going to smoke next.

35. You are free to stop worrying about successfully completing the enlightenment program (enjoy it!).

36. You are allowed to quit worrying about whether you will be able to "keep up" this good mood.

37. You are allowed to quit looking forward to when you can smoke again.

38. You are allowed to quit feeling guilty because you've just had a smoke.

39. You are allowed to quit feeling guilty for stopping work in order to go have a smoke.

40. You are allowed to quit worrying about the money you've already spent on trying to stop.

41. You are free to stop being so macho (or feminist, or aggressively defensive) about your smoking habit.

42. You are free to look at other smokers with nonjudgmental compassion.

43. You are free to look at anti-smokers with bemused indifference.

44. You are free to think of yourself as something larger and more profound than being a smoker or a nonsmoker.

45. You are free not to think about smoking at all.

46. You are allowed to abandon all of your beliefs about smoking and not smoking.

47. You are allowed to enjoy changing your relationships with all your smoking friends and with all your nonsmoking friends, regardless of whether you smoke.

48. You are free to live your life, think your thoughts, moment by moment, hour by hour, day by day, according to your own vision.

49. You are allowed to set the pace and direction of your own thinking, no matter where you are or who you are with.

50. You are free to laugh at yourself and enjoy your whole history with smoking and not smoking.

Now that you've quit all that, let's talk about some other tobacco traditions.

12 Getting Ready to Quit, Again and Still . . .

Purifying Your Daily Smoking Routines

> Dislodging a green nut from its shell is almost impossible, but let it dry and the lightest tap will do it.
>
> —Ramakrishna

We've already suggested the basic exercises that (if you actually do them!) will make your transition out of smoking much easier, more natural, and more effortless than you ever dreamed possible. You've enjoyed smoking for a number of years, now you are free to enjoy *not* smoking. Whether you're smoking or not smoking, you never have to give up joy.

Let's apply this theme to the next step in the more traditional methods for quitting. In *Quit*, Charles F. Wetherall suggests that those who are preparing to quit keep a written record of their daily smoking—how many cigarettes you smoke and when. He further suggests that you "rank" each of your cigarettes according to how important each one is to you. He suggests using a scale of 1 to 3, a 3 being a cigarette that is most important, and a 1 being a cigarette you simply smoke out of habit, unconsciously. (See Chapter 10 for other Wetherall suggestions.)

From an enlightened perspective, because you know that enjoying your happiness is the most important thing for you and for all those around you, you can follow Wetherall's suggestion and know that the cigarettes that are most important to you are the ones you enjoy *most*. The intent of Wetherall's suggestion is obvious: It should help you eliminate those cigarettes that are least important to you.

In other words, if the first cigarette you smoke with your first cup of coffee of the day is most important to you—if it's the one you most enjoy—and the fourth cigarette with your third cup of coffee is the least important, the least enjoyable, then Wetherall suggests that you begin by eliminating that fourth cigarette. If you want to follow his advice while using the enlightened approach, you would eliminate those cigarettes you didn't enjoy. And when you were tempted to smoke anyway, you'd remember, "Oh yes, I usually don't enjoy smoking a fourth cigarette with a cold cup of coffee," or whatever.

However, the enlightened approach is even easier! You should be clear that "important" is synonymous with "enjoyable" in this context. When you say that your first cigarette in the morning, or the one with the coffee, or the one with your evening cocktail is important to you, you suggest that these are the cigarettes that bring you the most enjoyment. Therefore, when you make a connection between the importance of smoking (i.e., the need for or authority of smoking) and your enjoyment of smoking, then the importance of smoking—as well as its authority of and the need for it—becomes relaxed. When you say a cigarette at a particular time and place is important to you, you simply respond to your need for happiness, which is itself quite healthy.

Wetherall's suggestion to track your smoking habits by recording when you smoke (the time), where you smoke (the place), and then the cigarette's rank (1–3) undoubtedly serves to heighten your awareness of your daily smoking patterns, which in turn makes each smoke a more conscious activity.

"Just being aware of the habit is enough to kick the habit," Wetherall suggests. We might refine his insight by saying, "Just *enjoying* the habit is enough to master the habit!"

As we mentioned, Wetherall's strategy for quitting is to begin cutting back on smoking by cutting out the least important cigarettes, then the moderately important cigarettes, and finally the most important cigarettes. The enlightened strategy is *not* to cut out the least and moderately important cigarettes, but rather to *transform* these into the most important cigarettes. You want to make every cigarette you smoke a deeply enjoyable, thoroughly satisfying experience.

"The cigarette you truly enjoy," asserts Dr. Almayrac (an M.D.!), "does not hurt you." Dr. Almayrac is deeply confident in the power of joy to mitigate any and all adverse consequences of smoking. This is truly a radical (and quite enjoyable) view! So the reason you begin to record and rank your daily cigarettes is so that you can make smoking *every* cigarette a truly enjoyable, important activity.

Back to tradition.

Wetherall suggests eliminating one cigarette each day starting with the least important. For instance, he would suggest that if you normally have three cigarettes with your first cup of coffee and the third cigarette is rated a "low 1," then that's the cigarette to eliminate. In our enlightened approach, the third cigarette would be the one you consciously strive to enjoy. Turn 1s into 3s! (As you will discover, the more you enjoy your smokes, then naturally, spontaneously, the fewer you'll need.)

Exercises

For the purposes of enjoying all of your smokes, and turning all of your 1s into 3s, here's a "starter list" of twenty-five suggestions you might follow to enjoy your smoking more.

1. You could buy a fancy cigarette case (or two or three) to keep your cigarettes in, to "honor" them for the joy they bring to you. If you can't afford to buy such a case (or two or three such cases, for different times and moods and dress), then you might consider *making* such cases. Yes, keeping your cigarettes in such cases might slow you down as you reach for a smoke. But when you slow down, you might more easily remember to enjoy what you are about to do!

2. Occasionally (or just once!), in the privacy of your home or car, you might allow yourself to fondle, kiss, coo, cuddle, smell, even *lick* your cigarette packs. Why not? Such "blasphemy," such indulgence, such open-hearted pleasure in your smoking instruments is a healthy outward acknowledgement of inner conditions. When you allow such feelings—such a relationship—to be expressed in your outer world, you may find the inner force of these feelings diminishes tenfold. With such open-hearted honesty, mastery ensues!

3. On occasion, you might carry your cigarettes in two hands cupped together, as though you are carrying an offering or precious commodity. The lessons you are

learning from your smoking may indeed be some of the most precious jewels you will ever receive. You can honor your smokes and your smoking this way. The honor will be returned!

4. You could praise, extol, glorify your particular brand of smokes, regardless of the logic or truthfulness behind such praise. For example: "Marlboro is the Choice of Intellectuals and Beauty Queens!" This is part of enjoying all that you are and all that you do, including selecting a cigarette brand.

5. You could consciously collect and enjoy different brands of tobacco so that you can combine them with other things. For example, you might have one brand with your coffee, another with different foods and drinks, another with desserts. Allow yourself to be a true connoisseur of various tobacco combinations. (You already enjoy such combinations, just make it a more conscious activity.)

6. You might allow extra time—at work, or before work, or before going to bed—to smoke an extra cigarette. To consciously create more time and space for a smoke, in which you strive to enjoy every thought and feeling, will quickly lift an unimportant to an important cigarette.

7. You might choose to smoke when and where you otherwise (or at least in the past) haven't smoked, such as while walking or exercising or even in the shower! (Yes, it can be done!) In the Enlightenment Game, you're *playing* with your smoking patterns, freely changing, rearranging, enjoying yourself with your smokes.

8. Playing this way, you might consciously decide to double your smoking one day—from one pack to two packs, or from half a pack to one pack. (Be sure to consciously enjoy all the thoughts and feelings that arise with such play, feeling guilty, crazy, etc.)

9. You could find new, perhaps "forbidden" places to smoke: in the elevator, the church balcony, the closet!

10. You can "stockpile" cigarettes. Maybe buy a whole case, or two cases. You may find tremendous joy, tremendous relief in spending your money for such a psychic "war chest." Your joy is the key!

11. You could start a list of all the things you enjoy about smoking and keep adding to it.

12. Sometime at home, just for fun, you could put out a slew of ashtrays in different rooms and for different "sitting places." Then, put an open pack beside each ashtray so you can go anywhere in the house and have a fresh smoke waiting for you, without carrying them around. What fun!

13. One day you might decide that smoking will be the most important thing you do that day. Give yourself permission to smoke—or take a smoke break—at every conceivable opportunity. When even the slightest thought of smoking crosses your mind, you'll do it! And you'll give yourself permission to drop everything else you're doing so that you can enjoy a smoke. Maybe you'll enjoy giving your-self three such "smoking days" every week, or at least one a month, or at least one some time. Honor the habit that has been such a faithful companion!

14. You could create a "smoking throne"—a favorite chair, or room, with special ashtrays, and lighters, and a special supply of expensive smokes, where you can smoke in absolute peace and majestic comfort.

15. At the right time, some evening or Sunday afternoon, you might decide to enjoy five cigarettes in a row. Slowly, perhaps, without rushing, but have one right after the other. Challenge yourself to enjoy the fifth as much as the first!

16. Some morning you might decide to see if you can smoke a whole day's worth of cigarettes before you get to work.

17. You could make a ritual out of the first cigarette you have after work. Prepare a place, a time, and make sure everything's set, every day for this ritual.

18. You can make your car into a "smoker's heaven," with extra smokes, matches, lighter, ashtrays, even a special bag to empty ashes in. Maybe use an air freshener, too. You smoke a lot in your car. You might as well enjoy it!

19. Select three cigarettes for your coffee break. Set them out on the table in front of you. Enjoy each cigarette completely, one at a time.

20. One day, carry three cigarettes with you wherever you go. The next day, carry just two cigarettes wherever you go. Enjoy the difference.

21. Set out two or three cigarettes for a telephone conversation with an old friend. Determining ahead of time these are the particular cigarettes you're going to smoke affirms your mastery, your autonomy, your *choice* in the matter.

22. Set out three or four cigarettes with your dinner, at the

side of your plate. You can take your time, enjoy your dinner, knowing these smokes are waiting.

23. When you buy your cigarettes, tell the person behind the counter, "I love these guys, I really do." Make no apologies, no excuses.

24. Sometime during the day, every day, talk to your cigarettes. Say, "I love you." And then in a different voice, pretend you're the cigarette talking back, "I love you, too [insert your name]." You can carry on a lover's conversation with your smokes, making up both sides. After all, to make a marriage work, you have to communicate. Or, if there is to be a divorce, it's best to make it amicable.

25. Every time you light up a smoke, start to hum or sing, whatever tune that happens to pop into your mind or one favorite tune you enjoy. Such spontaneous song is a sign to yourself, to your body, to the world at large, that you're ready to enjoy and are enjoying this activity. Why not? There's no law against humming while you smoke.

Again, these are just suggestions to prime the pump, to get *your* own personal ideas flowing on how to enjoy *your* smoking more regularly, more consistently. The idea is to totally, completely enjoy smoking, with no holding back, no half-hearted, halfway measures. These are the steps you must follow to master smoking, just as such full indulgence—full enjoyment!—is necessary to master anything, from golf to gardening.

The true point of these exercises, however, is not so much to help you enjoy smoking more, which is only the surface motivation. The goal of these exercises is to encourage you to enjoy yourself more, in all that you do. And more specifically, to enjoy yourself even while doing something that feels strange or forbidden.

When you reach that point when you're tired of smoking and smoking games (believe it or not, you will be!) and you're ready to move into the smoke-free season of your life, the first days and weeks will feel somewhat foreign or forbidden, just like these exercises. However, just as you find ways to enjoy these exercises, you will likewise find joy in the tobacco-free exercises that follow your quit date, whether it be today or a month or six months from now.

Do, Say, and Think Only What You Enjoy

Prior to simplifying the Enlightenment Exercise into its present form, Dr. Almayrac experimented with a form that he summarized with the declaration and observation, "I do not need to think anything, or say anything, or do anything that I am not happy to think or say or do." Over a period of time, practicing this form, he came to realize that he always had some thought before he either talked or acted. So he discovered that if he always *thought* what he was happiest thinking, he would necessarily say what he was happiest to say and *do* what he was happy to do. In this light, you can more clearly perceive how these exercises—these actions and sayings—are only the outward manifestations of enjoying your thoughts and feelings.

The activities previously suggested will only be useful and empowering if and when they are enjoyed. Without joy, there is no point and no value to them. As we've said before, it is not the activities themselves that lead to mastery of the smoking process, but the joy you experience in doing the activities.

This leads us to the consideration of consistency in this whole process. In his book on quitting, Wetherall insists that, "Once you eliminate a cigarette, YOU CAN'T GO BACK TO IT. Thus, if you give up the cigarette you have always had with your morning coffee, you want to forever stop smoking that cigarette."

Now, as you know, some mornings you feel a little brighter, a little snappier (more enlightened!) than you do on other mornings: Monday morning versus Saturday morning, for instance. With the Enlightenment Game, you are more and more ready to meet the day—whatever day it is—but still, some mornings feel more conducive to play than others. So on some mornings you may enjoy not smoking with your coffee. Other mornings, you enjoy smoking with your coffee. The only demand for consistency in the enlightened approach is your adherence to joy.

What the World Yearns For

Some days you may *not* want to think about your smoking at all. Some days you just don't want to deal with it, and you don't want to play with it or work with it, either. So be it! When you don't enjoy what you're doing, then you're not doing anything useful, even if you're refraining from smoking or if you're washing the dishes or mopping the floor. Joy is what this world yearns for—not just more dishes washed or floors mopped.

The only consistency required of you is a consistent adherence to your own inner happiness. Happiness is your true nature, your inner self, your highest ideal. When you remain true to your inner happiness, you remain true to yourself, to your highest ideals. By living your life this way, all those around you will benefit.

Such consistency to your happiness doesn't mean that you will necessarily be gleeful all the time, but you will indeed find you have more gleeful hours and days than you have ever had before. Some days you will be happy to be quiet, calm, contemplative; other days you will be happy to be more outgoing, exuberant; still other days you might be happy to be somewhere in-between. Your joy leads you to the right expression at the right time.

When you have practiced enjoying yourself in all your different smoking situations, and all of your non-smoking situations, and your practice has led you to a point where you are able to move more quickly out of your unhappiness, and are able to remain consistently in your happiness (what wonderful, enlightened training this is!), you are then ready to design a workable "quit day."

Don't worry! It'll be a lot more fun, more liberating and freeing than you might think. Read on....

13 Transcendental Nicotine Fits
How to Avoid (or Reduce) All Withdrawal Symptoms!

> There's nothing either good or bad but thinking makes it so.
> —William Shakespeare

Okay, you're almost ready for quit day. But it will be helpful to do just a little more pre-quit work, so that it really is an easy, enjoyable process.

We're on the downhill side of this book. I trust that, so far, it has given you a radical, yet very natural, very honest view of your smoking. Now we're cruising toward the finish line.

Since you're so close to quitting, in this chapter we're going to look at withdrawal and—as you might have guessed!—how you can enjoy the days or weeks immediately following quitting. Many smokers have found that they are able to use the Enlightenment Exercise in such a way that they do not experience any withdrawal symptoms at all! And if it's possible for them, it's possible for you!

INSIGHT *Here's the key: If you are enjoying your withdrawal experiences, enjoying your withdrawal symptoms, then you do* not *experience any withdrawal pains.*

However, not having any withdrawal symptoms is not our objective. As we have said time and time again, the objective is to enjoy yourself, every day, with or without smoking. If you experience withdrawal symptoms, but you enjoy them, then there's no problem, right? So the easiest approach is simply to decide that you are going to enjoy whatever your experience is. You are free to do this!

The American Psychiatric Association (APA) has identified a handful of common withdrawal symptoms that are often observed when someone stops smoking. The most common of these symptoms are a slowing of the heart rate, an increase in blood pressure, and modest changes in brain wave patterns (alpha, beta, theta). In what the APA terms "heavily addicted" smokers, a drop in body temperature may also occur with cessation of tobacco use. In what the APA terms "less addicted smokers," the body temperature may rise with cessation of smoking.

Empirical tests indicate that smokers going through nicotine withdrawal score less well in manual coordination tests, including driving, than they did when they were smoking. Researchers also report an increased incidence of mouth ulcers in those who quit and, on occasion, more pronounced effects such as becoming extremely hoarse, an increase in asthmatic conditions, or a heightening of sexual appetite. Many smokers experience more intense coughing spells after they quit, as their lungs begin to regain their sensitivity. But of course, the most common, most uncomfortable, and most forceful withdrawal symptom of all is a severe craving for tobacco. In the first days and weeks after quitting, this last symptom causes many smokers to return to tobacco use.

Other common symptoms, often contradictory, include irritability, hunger cravings, lack of ability to concentrate, sleeplessness, sleepiness, lethargy, and hyperactivity. Studies have shown that when they give up smoking different smokers experience some or all of these withdrawal symptoms to different degrees and for different lengths of time, during the first three days to two weeks and for up to two months after quitting.

These withdrawal symptoms are mentioned here to assure you that we are not naive or uninformed about what is "supposed" to happen, from a traditional point of view, when smokers quit smoking.

Having outlined these symptoms, however, I am delighted to inform you that more and more students of the enlightened approach to quitting are not experiencing *any* of these symptoms, at least not in an unpleasant fashion. And more and more frequently, the withdrawal symptoms that students experience are brief, fleeting, and easily eliminated with the techniques and exercises suggested here. Good news, isn't it?

As you know, the enlightened approach to quitting is based on your natural ability to immediately access your own native happiness. Your happiness, your joy, is the key to eliminating withdrawal symptoms. Your native happiness can naturally overpower any unpleasant symptoms that may arise. Smokers not only in my program, but in others around the world, have proven this, time and time again. This is your chance to prove it in your own life!

It is worth repeating that the primary goal of this book is to help you access your happiness more consistently and more deeply. By practicing the Enlightenment Exercise, you will find that you enjoy your life more deeply than ever before. Indeed, quitting smoking is only our secondary goal, and quite often it is simply the spontaneous by-product of accomplishing the first goal successfully.

As you begin practicing the Enlightenment Exercise in earnest—as you practice enjoying your thoughts, your feelings, your actions, and choosing to think only the thoughts, feel only the feelings, and perform only the actions you enjoy—you begin dissipating and side stepping all withdrawal symptoms even *before* you quit smoking!

Let's take a closer look at how this works. And let's begin with the most common, most forceful, and seemingly the most dangerous of all withdrawal symptoms: the intense craving for tobacco that occurs almost immediately when a smoker gives it up.

The Intense Craving

What we have consistently observed in our work with smokers is that *every* withdrawal symptom associated with stopping smoking is present even *before* you quit smoking. The best example of this is the intense craving for tobacco that seems most obvious after you quit. In other words, the intense craving for tobacco you might experience when you quit is not a new experience for you. In fact, it is the same craving that has kept you reaching for your cigarettes ten, twenty, or thirty or more times a day for years. You are already familiar with it, so you have already had sufficient opportunity to learn how to dissolve it.

But what is a craving? Try to notice it in your own smoking life. Isn't it simply a repetitive, insistent thought? You will discover that when you consciously begin to enjoy more and more of your thoughts—not only about tobacco but also about everything else in your life—you automatically begin to enjoy, and thus dissipate and dissolve, what before you have perceived as a craving. If you don't enjoy that thought, that craving, you'll do anything—including reaching for a smoke—to get rid of it. In fact, that's what you do right now. But if you *do* enjoy the thought, the craving, then it doesn't demand that you do anything about it.

You've probably discovered in your past attempts at quitting that soon after you decide, "That's it. No more. That was my last one!" you thereafter begin thinking about smoking continually. Many smokers return to smoking time and time again, after vowing not to, simply to escape the recurring, unpleasant thoughts about smoking that are as annoying and troubling as a swarm of hornets buzzing around their heads. At the time, it seems as though the only way to escape is to smoke. In other words, if you start to smoke again, you don't have to *think* about smoking.

However, many students of the enlightenment process discover that once they have consciously determined to enjoy all of their thoughts—no matter what the thoughts happen to be—and have practiced sufficiently before trying to quit, the process of stopping smoking can be completed without undue difficulty. The difficulty and discomfort of stopping smoking originates in the mental chamber, not the body. When you bring light, joy, and happiness to your mental chamber, the difficulty and discomfort disappear.

For example, the thought, "I want a cigarette," or "I need a cigarette," does not have to be difficult or uncomfortable or irritating, even though it repeats itself, perhaps hundreds of times, after you quit. Here's the key: The thought, "I need a cigarette," does not have to be acted on in order to be enjoyed!

You can play with the thought, as we discussed in Chapter 2. You can make it larger, smaller, brighter, dimmer. You can move it into your little toe, put it on the shelf, or transform it into a small child's handwriting or a frog's voice. Anything goes!

What happens to smokers who try to quit the old way is that they become *afraid* of these thoughts—the hornets—buzzing around in their heads. Bo Lozoff, director of the Prison Ashram Project and author of the best-selling *We're All Doing Time* and *Just Another Spiritual Book,* describes fear as

…a demon with boons [abilities] and curses. . . . One of the boons fear seems to have is the ability to take almost any form—the power of disguise. . . . Fear also has the boon of proximity and the boon of speed. What I mean by that is that fear has been given the power to get like a millionth of an inch away from our faces, and go "BOOO! BOOOO! ARGGGHHHHH!" [makes threatening and menacing noises], and it's been given power to talk really fast, like, "Watch out, watch OUT, WATCHOUTWATCHOUTWATCHOUT…."

But fear also has a couple of curses, a couple of limitations. The main one is that it cannot actually touch us. It can only get close, and pretend to touch us. It actually can never touch. And the other which is related to that, is that it can't make us do a damn thing. It doesn't have the power. It can only try to scare us into doing what it wants us to do.

So that's the demon known as fear. For example, you're a recovering alcoholic. You're in a situation where there's a lot of booze, and it's been a bad day, and you begin simultaneously feeling that desire to drink and also the fear that comes with it. And the demon fear starts using its powers. First of all, it gets RIGHT UP TO YOUR FACE. Then it starts using the power of speed and saying, "YOU'RE GOING TO DO IT DO IT, YOU'REGONNADOIT, GONNADOIT, GONNA-DOIT!" And because we are afraid of being overwhelmed by fear, we find ourselves reaching for the damn drink to get it over with, because it has scared us into thinking that we're going to do it anyway, and we may as well stop lying to ourselves, and we can't take this, we're just not strong enough, etc.

Sound familiar? When you learn to enjoy the thoughts that are coming through, you can even learn to enjoy your fears (and thus be fearless!).

We'll come back to this phenomenon—enjoying a thought without acting on it. But now, let's quickly review the other symptoms associated with withdrawal, and look at the experiences you can expect to have.

Other Symptoms

Heart Palpitations

Let's start with heart palpitations. Is there a single smoker who has not experienced heart palpitations at different times when smoking? That is, after all, one of the contradictory effects of nicotine. You have heart palpitations—either when you deny the body nicotine or when you add nicotine— because in both cases your body is responding to a new chemical balance. As a smoker, you have already learned to simply wait, allow the palpitations to diminish, and then continue on with your business. You generally don't freak-out with the onset of palpitations when you smoke. In fact, you have probably already learned secretly to enjoy these palpitations! They do, after all, give you a little rush of energy, a little high, a momentary distraction in your day. So, in fact, you might look forward to heart palpitations in the quitting process, rather than dreading them.

Brain-Wave Patterns

The same holds true with changes in your brain-wave patterns. You have three primary types of brain-wave patterns: beta, alpha, and theta. Beta waves are most prevalent when you are taking care of your everyday business, doing your shopping, or figuring your income tax. Alpha waves are most prevalent when you are relaxed, letting go, not so concerned with the hustle and bustle. Theta waves are associated with the dreaming state, when you have relaxed to a point of transcending your physical body altogether. (A fourth pattern—the delta wave—is associated with deep sleep, when there is no dreaming going on, at least within the body. A fifth pattern—the gamma wave—is associated with the highest, "peak experience" state of consciousness.)

All of these brain-wave patterns are present all of the time, but one or the other is dominant. As you already know, tobacco smoking is one way you have learned to change your brain-wave patterns. For example, you have a smoke to wake up, which changes the emphasis from theta and delta patterns to beta patterns. Later in the day, you smoke to relax, which changes the focus from beta patterns to alpha patterns. You smoke before going to sleep, which changes the emphasis from alpha to theta. Your smoking allows you to induce all types of variations—you smoke to concentrate, or to let go, to be sociable or to be alone, because you're hungry or because you're full. Each of these "states" has a different brain-wave pattern.

So, is it any wonder that researchers have discovered changes in brain-wave patterns when you quit? Especially during the first two or three days, you may find yourself floating in and out of all types of brain states, because, in fact, you have untethered the balloon! You have set yourself—and your brain-wave activity—free! So what should you do about these changes in brain-wave patterns?

Right! Enjoy!

Sure, if you have a cigarette you can start to bring the balloon back into a habitual holding pattern, but there's no reason you can't simply enjoy the ride. You'll soon discover (if you haven't already!) that without cigarettes you enjoy yourself more than you ever did with them. And that's the best (and most enlightened!) reason of all to quit!

Body Temperature

So what about the slight rise or fall in your body temperature, which is also a withdrawal symptom? As a smoker, you have learned to use tobacco to maintain the right climate in your body. You experience a slight rise or fall in body temperature when you light up, depending on the time and place. When you smoke, you enjoy it, and then either take off a sweater or put one on. The same should be true when you quit. Enjoy the changes—enjoy the feelings of your body coming alive again. And if you feel cold, put on a sweater. If you feel hot, take something off or turn on a fan. If you get cold, then hot, within a matter of minutes, enjoy it! Sure, it's not usual, but then, lighting a poisonous plant on fire twenty times a day, drawing the smoke into your lungs, and blowing it out is not all that usual either! So far, you haven't minded unusual. That's why you can learn to enjoy unusual temperature variations when you quit. Such variations won't last long—a matter of days, at most. So enjoy them while you can!

Coordination

Researchers have noted an initial decrease in manual coordination with cessation of tobacco use. As far as your manual coordination is concerned, how many times have you simultaneously coordinated your smoke, your drink, the telephone, and maybe your cat who needs to be fed? Would you be more coordinated with or without your cigarette and ashtray? Or how about when you're driving your car, trying to light a cigarette, and open the ashtray, and keep your eyes on the road? Would you be more coordinated with or without the cigarette?

When researchers suggest that your manual coordination will diminish briefly when you quit smoking, they are not giving enough commonsense credence to the fact that when you stop smoking you have two hands available rather than one to perform whatever task you need to do. Are you more coordinated (i.e., able to perform tasks better) with or without a cigarette in your hand? As far as your physical coordination is concerned, you are going to love not having a cigarette in your hand or mouth all the time. Sure, you might feel clumsy the first couple of days. So enjoy feeling clumsy! Prolong it, if you can! Without smoking, you are going to feel *immediately* more graceful, more in control. Just wait and see!

Sexual Appetite

Occasionally, researchers have discovered, sexual appetite increases when smoking ceases. So, is smoking sexy or not?

Remember, the symptom that arises from quitting is present before you quit. Almost every smoker is aware of the link—

consciously or subconsciously—between smoking and their sexuality. Many people begin smoking because they feel that smoking in some way will enhance their sexuality, or because a love interest is also smoking or thinks smoking is sexy. The increased sexual appetite results not only from the body coming alive, but because you feel better about yourself, you think better about yourself, you feel more sexy and more alive.

Many smokers quit because smoking is no longer considered as sexy as once it was. But the link between smoking and sex is not a mystery. As smokers or nonsmokers begin enjoying themselves, enjoying their thoughts and feelings, they naturally begin also enjoying other people more. And it is this joy—this natural enjoyment of yourself and your ability to enjoy those around you—that is the essence of attractiveness, of sexiness, and not simply whether you smoke or don't smoke. Practicing the Enlightenment Exercise will make you feel very attractive and will in fact make you more attractive! Whether that's of interest to you or not, it's something that will happen! So be prepared for second glances!

Weight Gain

Surprisingly, the symptom that most smokers dread is increased hunger, which seems inevitably to lead to some degree of weight gain. We'll talk about this excuse for not quitting in more detail in Chapter 18, but let's take a brief look here.

"I used to be very strict about my diet," says Dr. Almayrac. "I used to follow what is considered to be a very pure diet—no meat, no dairy, no sweets. Now, I eat what I enjoy. And I have never felt better."

Geneen Roth, author of many best-selling books including *Breaking Free from Compulsive Eating* and *When Food Is Love,* is at the forefront of the latest nutritional theory. She believes that our own inner "joy" is a sufficient and effective guide to eating. Sondra Ray, in her book, *The Only Diet There Is,* suggests that the only diet necessary for proper weight maintenance is a "mental diet," that is, abstaining from unhappy thinking. These and other metaphysical researchers have proven that weight problems come about not because we enjoy food too much or because we enjoy eating, but rather because we are unhappy with ourselves and use eating as a way to escape or to numb ourselves. Often, food is the *only* way we have learned to pleasure and enjoy ourselves.

We get trapped into the overeating habit—just like we get trapped into the cigarette habit—when what we enjoy with one breath we deny and berate ourselves for in the next breath. We can enjoy eating, and we can enjoy not eating. When we learn to enjoy all our thoughts about eating, however, we will have discovered the best diet there is.

Trust your joy! You may enjoy putting on five or ten pounds or more as a reward to yourself for quitting smoking. But if you stick with your joy, you will discover that you also enjoy taking those pounds off again; or you may discover that your joy in other things in life is so great that food is no longer your only pleasure. Practicing the Enlightenment Exercise, you find yourself taking pleasure in simply waking up in the morning. Your life simplifies, beautifies, in every way as you learn to honor your native happiness. Part of that beauty will be your physical shape—just watch!

Miscellaneous Symptoms

How about the physical symptoms, such as more coughing, mouth ulcers, and eye watering? They may, indeed, intensify when you quit smoking. That is because your body, without the continuing introduction of carbon monoxide and other toxins, is coming alive! It is regenerating, finding its new balance!

And yet, again, coughing, mouth ulcers, and watering of the eyes are certainly not uncommon for smokers. In fact, aren't they common symptoms for smokers? So if you should experience these symptoms when quitting, perhaps with more intensity than you are accustomed to, it is because these processes are working their way out of the body altogether! You can enjoy such cleansing or, at the very least, the *idea* of such cleansing. Knowing what's happening, you don't need to struggle against the symptoms— they're good for you!

Practicing the Enlightenment Exercise, you spontaneously begin enjoying your body more, because you are not badgering it with unhealthy thoughts or loading it down with heavy feelings. Enjoying your thoughts is the healthiest thing you can do for yourself. And it will show in your body.

Withdrawal Exercises

1. In your smoking journal, name the three withdrawal symptoms you most worry about.
2. Now, write out three thoughts that you can enjoy thinking about each symptom.
3. Name two withdrawal symptoms that you can look forward to.

4. Take five minutes and write a description of what it would be like for you to die from cigarette withdrawal. Be as descriptive as you can.
5. Take ten minutes and describe what it would be like for you to quit smoking without any withdrawal symptoms whatsoever. Be as descriptive as you can.

You might as well prepare yourself for a delightful time, yes? In the next chapter, we'll look at your upcoming quit day and how to make it easy, natural, graceful.

14 Quit Day Coming...
One Way or Another!

> To reach the port of Heaven we must sail sometimes with the wind and sometimes against it. But we must sail [with our thoughts] and not drift or lie at anchor.
> —Oliver Wendell Holmes

When people learn I'm a stop-smoking teacher, they are often anxious to tell me how *they* stopped smoking. The traditional "old school" way of quitting was recently recounted to me by a retired elevator mechanic. This fellow had been a two-pack-a-day smoker. While working on the elevator at a local hospital, he had a heart attack, during which his breathing stopped and his heart went into fibrillation. Because he was at the hospital when it happened, he was immediately given mouth-to-mouth resuscitation followed by defibrillation to return his heart to a normal rhythm, after which they took him, still unconscious, into surgery where they did an emergency double-bypass operation. Had he not been in the hospital at the time of his attack, he probably would have died. He finally returned to consciousness two days later.

"I haven't wanted a smoke since," he said, quite proud.

"Hearing angel feathers" is one way of quitting smoking. Many smokers have quit this way. This book outlines a more graceful (joyful!), less trauma-filled approach.

As you practice the Enlightenment Exercise and find the energy surrounding your own smoking starting to loosen and shift around, it's natural that you're going to start thinking about your quit day—the day when you finally completely expel the habit from your life. As we mentioned earlier, you don't have to think of your quit day with fear and loathing. Start to think of it with thoughts you enjoy. Make the actual thoughts, or the series of thoughts, of your quit day *brighter* than they have ever been. Make them colorful, expansive, large. How you literally *think* about your quit day is how it literally will be! As you begin to enjoy the thoughts surrounding this event, then you will set yourself up to enjoy it. And when you enjoy the event, there is simply no way it can fail.

Again, let's get some perspective on what you are doing here. It is *not* quitting smoking that is your life's purpose. Rather, the purpose of your life is to love and enjoy and grow. So instead of asking you to set a quit date for smoking, we suggest you first set a quit day for any and every thought you are not happy to think or feel. Isn't this what you and all of us are most fundamentally seeking: a day of complete peace and happiness? To refrain from all thoughts that you are not happy thinking is the highest discipline and the most healthful of all abstinences!

Here's the paradox: Quitting tobacco will remove one of the primary activities in your life, which tends to lead you to think thoughts you don't enjoy. But, thinking thoughts you enjoy about tobacco makes it easier to quit. So your primary quitting, your most important quit day in fact, will be when you stop thinking thoughts you don't enjoy.

Tell yourself, "Today I am giving up thinking any thoughts I don't enjoy." With this focus, even if you aren't one hundred percent successful on your first day of quitting, or even if you're only ten percent successful your first day or two percent successful, you'll find it very enticing to take up the discipline again the next day, because even a two percent success rate makes your whole day brighter. This is the type of quitting that is enjoyable to return to time and time again until you succeed.

So rather than counting how many cigarettes you smoked today, you can look to see how successful you were at enjoying all of your thoughts today. As you take up this discipline, you may or may not quit smoking cigarettes right away. But if you do decide to quit smoking with this frame of mind, you'll discover the quitting process is absolutely trouble-free.

This approach is designed to help you become one of the people Charles Wetherall describes in *Quit* when he writes, "others seem to face no battle whatsoever. They sail through the quitting experience with little or no thought at all—even without altering their lifestyle." Such an experience arises for people when they understand that they have smoked simply because they enjoyed smoking and that they are now quitting simply because they want to enjoy quitting.

Again, Wetherall points out, "Quitting cigarettes is a *process* rather than a simple event or act . . . it is not 'willpower' that spells the difference in successfully giving up cigarettes but rather *our commitment to learn new behavior or replace old*" (emphasis added).

Your *"commitment to learning new behavior"*—to learning this new way of processing your thoughts—will occur in direct proportion to your perception and acceptance of the truth contained in the Law of Happiness: *Enjoying my happiness is the most important thing for me and for everybody around me.* This is the new principle, the new behavior you want to learn. (It's like asking you to make a commitment to eating strawberry pie. This is a *delightful* new behavior to learn!)

When the thought, "I want a cigarette" arises, you simply allow yourself to enjoy the thought, enjoy the feeling. You don't need to fight the thought, nor do you need to act on it. You simply enjoy yourself, and then enjoy the next feeling, the next thought, whatever it happens to be.

If your next thought is "I shouldn't smoke. I told myself I wouldn't," then simply enjoy that thought. Or, if you can't enjoy it, then change it into something you do enjoy.

 Whether you smoke or don't smoke is not the criterion for your success. Your joy is the only criterion.

The Commitment Required

"If your commitment is there," writes Wetherall, "you'll do whatever is necessary to quit smoking. If your commitment is not there, completing even the first step of this program will be too much of a challenge."

The only commitment required in the enlightenment approach is a commitment to thinking what you most enjoy thinking. Without such commitment, your attempts to master your smoking are more likely to be hard, slow, and painful. Commitment to your happiness is the key to success in mastering smoking.

So Wetherall's words might read instead, "If your commitment to your own happiness is there, you'll do whatever is necessary to enjoy quitting smoking. If your commitment to your own happiness is not there, then completing even the first step of this program will be too much of a challenge."

Let's continue with Wetherall's stop-smoking advice. "You can only quit one day at a time," he writes. ". . . You can quit only for this moment. . . . Many quitters, in fact, concern themselves not with a day at a time, but rather an hour (or even a minute) at a time."

Again, Wetherall's focus is helpful, but with a slight change it becomes more useful. Our discipline is to enjoy ourselves, one *thought,* one *feeling* at a time. You aren't obliged to be happy for the rest of your life but, rather, to simply enjoy the thought, the feeling, you are experiencing right now.

The Moment You Quit . . .

"The first thing you'll notice when you quit smoking," says Wetherall, "is a sudden preoccupation with cigarettes and smoking."

You've undoubtedly experienced this: When you tell yourself you aren't going to smoke anymore, your thoughts are immediately drawn to that very subject. That's why we have repeatedly stressed to you the importance of enjoying *all* your thoughts about smoking. When you quit, all your thoughts about smoking come rushing in, so it makes the quitting process a lot more comfortable, a lot less distressing, when you have prepared yourself by learning to enjoy all of your smoking thoughts.

Using the enlightened approach, you allow yourself to experience this sudden preoccupation with smoking, which occurs when you decide to quit, as an enjoyable preoccupation, an enjoyable occurrence. In Chapter 13, we explored in detail the enlightened approach to the physical withdrawal symptoms that sometimes (but not always!) occur with the cessation of smoking. We demonstrated how these withdrawal symptoms—such as nervousness, inattention, preoccupation with smoking—are in fact the same symptoms you experience before quitting, simply because you are a smoker. So by the time you are ready to quit you're already an expert at handling withdrawal.

Despite the physical symptoms of withdrawal, which are in truth fairly minor irritants, the primary difficulty you experience when you quit is not in the body but rather in the mind, in the thoughts and feelings that you experience on the day when you decide to quit.

Here's how it happens: When you attempt to give some authority to the thought, "I've quit," or "I'm quitting,"—that is, when you hold onto the thought that you're going to quit—other thoughts immediately arise to challenge the truth and finality of such statements.

Your sudden preoccupation with smoking may come in the form of such thoughts as, "I can't do it. . . . Smoking's not that bad. . . . I'll quit later. . . . Who cares?. . . Who says so?. . . I'm not ready." And worse, perhaps the most common, most insistent, most repetitive thought of all begins: "Should I smoke or shouldn't I? Should I smoke or shouldn't I? Should I or shouldn't I?"

In his public presentations, Dr. Almayrac has often observed, "Everything in the universe wants to be loved [i.e., enjoyed]. When something comes to you which you do not love, it will keep coming back until you *do* love it."

Thus, the enlightened challenge before you is not to dismiss your thoughts about smoking or to overcome them or suppress them, but rather to simply enjoy them (however unusual this may seem!). For instance, when the question "Should I or shouldn't I?"

begins, the challenge is not to somehow give the right answer to the question, or to insist on the right outcome to the question, but rather to enjoy the question itself as it begins—enjoy yourself in the process of asking the question!

What to Do With the Thoughts

This is a perfect opportunity to employ some of the neurolinguistic thought programs we discussed earlier (see Chapter 2). When you think, "I need a cigarette," and you do not enjoy the thought, you might enjoy it more if you made it as big as a billboard, or as big as a building, silhouetted with fireworks against the night sky. You don't have to act on the thought, you just need to do something with it so that you enjoy it.

Or, when you think "I need a cigarette," you might just want to turn the brightness down on it. Make it dimmer; bring it to a staticky gray so the words are barely visible. You are free to do whatever you want with your thoughts.

Or, you may want to move the thought out of your head and into your small toe. "I need a cigarette" coming from your small toe is a lot less immediate, a lot less forceful than when the same thought is blasting away there behind your eyeballs.

You might want to give the thought an unenjoyable color—a pea green, maybe, or a dirty yellow. It's not that you are supposed to create unenjoyable thoughts. Rather, the suggestion is for you to *enjoy* dealing with a pesky, persistent thought, in a creative, unusual manner. Why not explode it into a million tiny pea-green or dirty-yellow pieces?

Whatever it takes for you to enjoy the thought, "I need a cigarette," do that! Maybe you want to put a frame around it, and then hang it on an interior wall. Or, once it's framed, throw it into an interior incinerator, or skip it across the thought sky like a frisbee, then change it into skywriting, and watch it slowly disappear. The point is, your joy is the authority, and you have the authority to enjoy all of your smoking thoughts in whatever way you can.

When you give authority to the thought, "I won't smoke anymore," all the other smoking thoughts that were seemingly "dethroned" and shut out by that authority immediately come knocking on the door, wanting to be reassured that they, too, are "loved" (i.e., enjoyed).

INSIGHT *For the thought, "I am quitting" or "I have quit," to remain in authority, you must empower that thought, that notion, with your own inner happiness. You must be happy to think, "I am quitting" or "I have quit." You must truly enjoy your thought, or the thought will have no power!*

So if you have decided to quit today, then you already know the answer to the question, "Should I or shouldn't I smoke?" When it comes back, as it will, time and again for a day or two, the challenge is not simply to give the right answer to that question ("No, I won't smoke") but to enjoy the question's continual arising.

INSIGHT *Your joy removes you from conflict.*

When you enjoy the question "Should I or shouldn't I smoke," joy will lead you automatically into the reasons you enjoy not smoking. Joy always leads to more joy. You will soon discover (if you haven't already!) that you are *enjoying yourself in the quitting process*.

The traditional approach of instilling power in thought is to pile up enough good reasons for quitting so that the "reactive" thoughts (such as "I can't!" or "I need it!") cannot tumble the authority of the "I quit!" thought.

Again, the enlightened approach is to love (enjoy!) all your thoughts, not only the "I quit" thought but also the "I'm not ready!" thought. In the enlightened approach, you are encouraged to enjoy the battle, enjoy the preoccupation, and the nervous energy. You can even enjoy the distraction that occurs when you decide to quit.

Wetherall and others suggest that you have "reasons for quitting" written out, ready, even memorized for when these "reactive" thoughts arise. If you have developed several reasons for quitting that you enjoy thinking about, time and time again, then writing them down and having them available is indeed valuable. A quick review or glance at your list through the day will reconnect you with your deeper joy and the added power you have for doing what you have set out to do.

And yet, even more powerful than having your list available is determining to employ the Enlightenment Exercise itself, where you consistently enjoy *all* your thoughts and consistently entertain only those thoughts that you enjoy. When you enjoy the thought, "I need a cigarette," you are master of that thought. It no longer drives you. In one moment you might enjoy that thought and in the next moment you might enjoy the thought, "I am free of cigarettes." With your natural happiness, you are allowed to enjoy these opposites, these contradictions and paradoxes.

As you enjoy the psychic tension created by these seemingly opposing thoughts, you'll discover that the tensions are soon dissipated. But remember, you don't enjoy it in order to dissolve it. You enjoy the tension simply because it is who you are, what you are in this moment. You enjoy all that you are, in every moment, as you move through the process of mastering tobacco addiction. Setting down your cigarettes then becomes effortless, graceful, pleasant.

Again, it is perfectly permissible and even advisable to have all of your reasons for quitting written out, clear and ready for your quit day. However, the authority, the power for quitting does not reside in these thoughts, these reasons, but in the joy you have in this moment as you think them. If you enjoy a thought one moment but receive no pleasure from it the next moment, simply drop it and think of a thought you *do* enjoy.

Most stop-smoking programs rely on the power of logic, the power of reason, to block or overcome the irrational desire to smoke. The enlightened path proposes that by loving (enjoying!) the irrational desire, you set it free, set it at peace. Thus, you are no longer at war with it and you are free.

What about the Future? And the Past?

One of the thoughts or series of thoughts that will probably come up for you to work with are those of a "smokeless" future. Or, on the other hand, you might have thoughts or see images of your past, about all your years smoking and all your previous attempts at quitting. Whether your thoughts are about the future or the past, they are still simply thoughts that you are experiencing (creating!) right now. Play the Enlightenment Exercise with them (i.e., *Do you enjoy your thought right now, yes or no? Anything other than a spontaneous "yes" is a "no."*)

"My past is not dead. It is alive," Dr. Almayrac says. "The

quality of the thought I have about my past right now determines the quality of my past." We've already discussed this notion in previous chapters. We've also mentioned the study done by the University of Ottawa that showed that most smokers who successfully walked away from their habits did so after attempting to quit three to five different times. Thinking about how many times you have tried to quit before can *empower* you, not deflate you.

"The thought we hold about our past determines our past," Dr. Almayrac observes, and the same holds true for the thoughts we hold about our future. It is the thought you hold right now that reveals your true past and future!

So do you have any thoughts about any of your previous quitting days? The more you enjoy your thoughts about your previous quit days or your previous attempts at quitting, the more you'll enjoy the present quit day! If you don't enjoy your thoughts about your previous attempts to quit, it's quite simple for you to enjoy them now. Take one thought at a time. What you did in the past was great, fun, exactly what you needed to do to bring you to where you are today!

We've already worked in-depth at finding reasons you can enjoy to quit smoking. Through this process, you are spontaneously creating an enjoyable future. You can make both your past and future enjoyable. This is the enlightened state of being!

Exercise

In your smoking journal, write out a beautiful, enjoyable script of thoughts you can think on your quit date. Make it easy, graceful, pleasurable. Write a script that makes your particular quit date the easiest, most graceful, most pleasant day in history. Why not? You are free to plan it just this way, and you deserve it!

As you approach your smoking and not smoking with this enlightened perspective, you discover that you are starting to "breathe easy"—not only about your smoking, but about your life in general. That's perfect. And breathing easy is exactly what is taken up in the next chapter, so, take a breath, and let's plunge on.

15 Breathing Joy!

> By working with your breath you are able to tune into the larger energies of the universe. Furthermore, there is an intimate relationship between thought and breath. When you calm [enjoy] your breath, there is a simultaneous calming [enjoying] of the mind.
>
> —Baba Ram Dass

SMOKER: I hear you've given up smoking. So what do you do instead?

EX-SMOKER: I *breathe*!

There's more to this response than first meets the eye, because there's more to breathing than you might think. An aspect of smoking that most authorities seem to overlook, and of which smokers themselves are often unaware, is the role that smoking plays in breath control!

Having been a smoker myself for many years, and having worked directly with many smokers of all ages and socioeconomic backgrounds and after *watching* smokers from afar—in restaurants, in their cars, at football games—it now seems obvious to me that smoking often functions as a lower form of yoga. Smoking is a way of regulating the breath that leads to a heightened or expanded state of consciousness.

Wait a minute. Smoking as a form of yoga? Precisely!

The sixth chapter of the *Bhagavad Gita*, one of the ancient scriptural texts of India, says:

When the restlessness of the mind, intellect, and self is stilled through the practice of Yoga, the yogi, by the grace of the Spirit within himself finds fulfillment. Then he knows the joy eternal which is beyond the pale of the senses which his reason cannot grasp. He abides in this reality and moves not therefrom. He has found the treasure above all others. There is nothing higher than this. He who has achieved it shall not be moved by the greatest sorrow. This is the real meaning of Yoga—a deliverance from contact with pain and sorrow.

Read the same passage but consider smoking as a form of yoga. For example, "When the restlessness of the mind, intellect, and self is stilled through the practice of *smoking,* the *smoking yogi,* by the grace of the Spirit [happiness!] within himself finds fulfillment."

Haven't you used smoking to "still the restlessness of the mind, intellect, and self," and to find the happiness, the fulfillment within? Sure—that's part of its appeal! That's what we've been pointing to throughout our reading together.

Is not the joy and contentment you feel when smoking an attraction that "reason cannot grasp?" Don't you *"abide in* [your smoking] *reality,"* and refuse to be moved therefrom? Haven't you considered your smoking a treasure that is as important to you as life itself? Hasn't it stayed with you through your greatest troubles and sorrows?

Let's not stretch the metaphor too far. But do recognize that smoking has offered you a regular and direct breathing practice that is similar to a form of yoga practice called *pranayama*, which means "rhythmic control of breath." The act of taking in smoke, holding it, and then letting it out slowly is identical (sans smoke) to various *pranayama* exercises. The density of the smoke makes it easier to feel the effects of such a breathing exercise, in the same way training wheels make it easier to learn how to ride a bike. Even though you may be ready to quit smoking, you surely aren't ready to quit breathing. So you need not quit enjoying your breathing, consciously using it in ways to help you relax, or to get fired up, or to move into a different state of consciousness. Continue to use your breathing for all the things you used smoking for in the past.

Paramahansa Yogananda reports:

The restless monkey breathes at a rate of 32 times a minute, in contrast with man's average of 18 times. The elephant, tortoise, snake, and other creatures noted for their longevity have a respiratory rate that is less than man's. The tortoise, for instance, which may attain the age of three hundred years, breathes only four times a minute.

B. K. S. Iyengar, in his classic book, *Light on Yoga,* says:

The normal rate of breaths per minute is 15. This rate increases when the body is upset by indigestion, fever, cold and cough, or by emotions like fear, anger, or lust. The normal rate of breathing is 21,600 breaths inhaled and exhaled every 24 hours. The yogi measures his span of life not by the number of days, but of breaths. Since breathing is lengthened in pranayama, its practice leads to longevity.

Continuous practice of pranayama will change the mental outlook of the practitioner and reduce considerably the craving of his senses for worldly pleasures like smoking, drinking, and sexual indulgence.

In the practice of pranayama the senses are drawn inward and in the silence of the kumbhaka (the stillness between breaths) the aspirant hears his inner voice calling: *"Look within. The source of all happiness is within."* (emphasis added)

Every professional singing or voice teacher will attest to the fact that in the West very few people in the general population consistently breathe properly, that is, deeply, rhythmically, consciously. Very few of us breathe with any degree of conscious attention as to the potential of what our breath is capable of doing.

In the Eastern tradition, experiments with breathing and instruction in breath control have been ongoing for close to five thousand years. Yogis have discovered that the breath is one of the basic keys to conscious regulation of the mind, the emotions, and the body. Elmer Green, from the highly regarded Meninger Clinic, conducted a series of studies with several different advanced yogis. The result was a significant body of clinical evidence showing that these "breath practitioners" are indeed capable of exerting conscious control over their heartbeat, blood flow, and autonomic nervous system. These yogis were able to minimize the experience of pain and maximize the body's endurance. (We've already discussed how nicotine provides very similar results!)

So unknowingly we've enjoyed smoking as a beginner's form of yoga. Where do we go from here, after we give up smoking? How might we best use the breathing process to move us through the first days and weeks after smoking and then in the future?

The Basic Breathing Exercise

Yogananda says:

A person whose attention is wholly engrossed, as in following some closely knit intellectual argument, or in attempting some delicate or difficult physical feat, automatically breathes very slowly. Fixity of attention depends on slow breathing; quick or uneven breaths are an inevitable accompaniment of harmful emotional states: fear, lust, anger.

Yoga practitioners throughout the centuries have developed literally thousands of different breathing rhythms and patterns for students to follow, to play and experiment with, each designed to move you into a particular state of consciousness, or to remove certain impurities, or to relieve certain ailments. The study of breath and breathing, and all of its variations, can be a life-long study.

The basic practice suggested by most teachers is to breathe smoothly, deeply, through your nose, pulling air down your "frontal column" to a point several inches below your navel; holding it for several counts, and then releasing the air as you imagine it traveling up your spinal column, around the head, and out; holding it again for several counts before breathing in. This is called the "circle of breath."

Various teachers have different approaches as to how many counts you should use for the in-breath and the out-breath. Some believe that the in-breaths and the out-breaths should be given equal time. Others think you need a bigger out-breath than in-breath or (more rarely) vice versa. Many teachers recommend that you spend time each day harmonizing your breathing with your heartbeat, breathing in for four or five or six heartbeats, then holding your breath for several heartbeats, and breathing out the same number of heartbeats.

You might already guess what we recommend for a basic breathing exercise: Just enjoy it! Right! When you consciously *enjoy* your breathing, one breath at a time, you are doing the most basic, yet also one of the most powerful, exercises possible.

The Formal Exercise

In yoga, the practice of *pranayama* is generally quite formal. The student is advised to devote a certain amount of time each day, at the same hour if possible, in the same place when practical, repeating the same routines. It is generally recognized that the early morning hours, before or as the sun is rising, are best suited for the first session of the day. (These exercises are generally not recommended for evening because they are, generally, quite energizing.)

When the basic routines are mastered, after a week or a month or a year or many years, then the next set of exercises is taken up, and again a regular schedule is engaged until these exercises are likewise mastered. Formal sessions can last anywhere from five minutes to an hour or more.

You can set up a similar "formal program," if you are so inclined, as you practice "joyful breathing." After having spent many years as a smoking yogi, practicing your smoking yoga, you will find it quite helpful and comforting to consciously reacquaint yourself with your natural, spontaneous breathing patterns.

The intention of such a program is to give your natural, ordinary breath some much-needed and deserved daily loving (joy!).

Consider your breathing a child who has not been given much attention during past years. You are now in the position of the absent parent who has come home to make amends for being away all these years. Give your breath some happy, daily quality time.

In the basic enlightened breathing exercise, you simply sit down, put your attention on your breath, and enjoy whatever breathing pattern naturally arises. In the Zen tradition, it is suggested that you count your breaths—count the out-breaths up to ten and then begin counting again. In other Buddhist traditions and in some of the Hindu traditions, it is suggested that you count up to one hundred or more breaths in a row. (One hundred eight is a sacred number in many traditions.) Or, you may just want to silently note, "Inhale, exhale."

At this point, your main intent is simply to enjoy your breath in whatever form it takes. Your own happiness may lead you to take up more traditional forms of yoga and explore the traditional breathing exercises that have been developed. For the purpose of finding freedom from tobacco, however, such practices are not necessary.

So when you sit down to simply enjoy your breath, if your breath happens to come shallow and fast, then enjoy shallow and fast! If it comes in spurts, enjoy spurts! If it comes in halting, ragged bursts, followed by long easy breaths, enjoy that! In these sessions, you need not try to make your breathing deep or rhythmical or even smooth. Whatever pattern your breathing takes in the moment, enjoy it! Make it easy on yourself.

When you determine to simply (and consciously!) enjoy your breath, you will discover that it takes on the pattern—the speed, the depth, the intensity—that is most conducive to harmony, and thus the form most helpful for you right now. Most likely, as you do sit to simply enjoy your breath, you will discover that your breath spontaneously begins to even out, get deeper, more regular, flowing in harmony with your thoughts and feelings, and even with your heartbeat!

These formal easy breathing sessions might accompany your morning prayer and meditation time, or your daily journal-writing sessions. As you engage in formal breathing sessions, you will discover that your informal breathing becomes much more conscious, harmonious, and refreshing.

Informal Exercises

Among the definitions Webster's dictionary gives for "inspiration" is "inhalation." To remain "inspired" throughout the day, placing your attention on your breath for the sole purpose of enjoying it can be very useful (as well as quiet and unobtrusive!). Returning attention to your breathing can be a "safe harbor" for your thoughts. It can be a way of returning your attention to joy. The admonition to "take a deep breath" before you plunge into something new is filled with the wisdom of the ages.

If you have been inspired to take up regular, formal, easy breathing, even if you don't do it every day as recommended, you will still discover that such *formal* exercise leads you into more regular *informal* attention to your breath and your breathing patterns (and thus to your joy!) throughout the day. You can train yourself to let your breath be the trigger that signals you to drop thoughts you don't enjoy or obsessive concerns with some subject in the past or the future, thereby bringing you back to joy in the present moment. As you remember your breath, you remember your joy.

The Enlightenment Exercise is designed to help you enjoy your thoughts throughout the day—moment by moment. When you place your thoughts on your breath (enjoying your breath!), you magnify the exercise and prepare yourself for whatever will come up next in this day, this hour, this minute.

Breathing and Withdrawal

You'll discover that if you enjoy your breath more consciously, more regularly (along with your thoughts!), you will be much less anxious, much less nervous, and much *more* empowered to simply move through the day without anxiety or discomfort when your quit day comes.

There's a simple physiological reason for this: When you are more aware of your breathing, when you enjoy your breathing more and thus spontaneously breathe more deeply, more regularly, you naturally bring more oxygen into your system. Oxygenating your system helps cleanse and detoxify your bloodstream and your vital organs and your cells. Breathing with joy helps you to revitalize your old smoking body more quickly.

Even more specifically, if you have learned to enjoy your breathing—either formally or informally—such joy can be a useful momentary fix when the craving (i.e., insistent thought) for a cigarette begins a day or two after you have quit. Your breathing is a convenient, natural place to focus your thoughts instead of on smoking. Enjoying a few deep or lazy breaths (quietly, unobtrusively) will sometimes help you drop your preoccupation with smoking so you can move on to whatever is next in your day's activities.

To suggest that breathing might be a viable (and sufficient!) alternative to smoking is not as far-fetched as it might seem when you realize that it was your breathing that you enjoyed—with the training wheels of smoke—all along. Breathing is not just a simple-minded, everybody-does-it affair. Some yogis are able to move immediately into a very blissful *samadhi*—an altered state of consciousness, a deeper enlightenment—simply by changing their breathing patterns (in conjunction with their thought patterns). Your breathing can be a powerful friend! What you may have been overlooking and down playing—that is, the simple fact that you are breathing—is a most wondrous and truly powerful companion that can help you move through the quit days with relative ease.

Formal breathing sessions, during which you regularly focus for a certain amount of time, whether started before or after your quit day, will help you engage the informal breathing exercises that, in conjunction with the enlightenment exercise, help dissolve withdrawal irritations.

So the instruction you are left with in this chapter? *Breathe*, my friend! Formally and informally, *breathe* and enjoy!

And if you find yourself accidentally taking another cigarette, lighting it and smoking it, even with all this help, what do you do then?

Breathe and enjoy! Formally and informally.

Exercise

1. Observe your natural "smoking breath." Do you inhale more deeply, or exhale more deeply? Do you ever hold your breath? If so, on the inhale or the exhale? How many

breaths does it take for you to smoke a cigarette? Keep track of this in your smoking journal. Watch what happens to your breathing as you practice joy!

2. Take time to count ten breaths, to *enjoy* ten breaths. Can you take this time easily, or is your mind like a "restless monkey"? Keep practicing enjoying your breathing, until you are an old, old person.

For a deeper look at what to do when you have a smoking relapse, please turn to the next chapter.

16 Falling Off the Mountain
Can I Have Just One?

> Stopping smoking's easy. I've done it hundreds of times.
> —Mark Twain

What happens if you have decided that you are not going to smoke? Your quit day arrives, and you have a dozen reasons—a dozen thoughts—that you truly enjoy when you think about not smoking anymore.

So you're on your way—the first hours, or days, or weeks have gone according to plan. You've told yourself you will be happy not to smoke anymore, for any reason, at anytime.

And then suddenly—*aaargh!*—for any one of a zillion reasons, you find that you "just had to have one." You didn't want to change your thoughts; you didn't want to out-breathe the urge; you didn't want to find something different to do with your mind and your lungs and your hands. You didn't want to do anything new or different or crazy or fun. You just wanted to have an old-time smoke. So you did it—you smoked a cigarette or two or three. What then? How do you proceed?

First, let's recall one thing: The "primary discipline," the "basic technique" in the enlightenment process is enjoying your thoughts. As radical as it might seem, quitting smoking—not having a cigarette—is only a secondary discipline, or a tertiary, a quadriary discipline. The most important thing is for you to enjoy your thoughts—enjoy yourself in all that you do! Just like learning to smoke, learning to quit smoking through the enlightenment process is a *season* you go through, not just a cliff you jump off.

INSIGHT *In this season of smoking cessation, the most dangerous form of backsliding is* not *simply smoking a cigarette. The most dangerous form of backsliding is* forgetting *to enjoy your thoughts.*

Remember, the success of this new approach you are adopting is measured in how much you enjoy yourself. Your stopping smoking will be a welcome side effect, but it's only a by-product of the primary discipline: joy!

So if you enjoy all of your thoughts, before, during, and after smoking a cigarette, can you have one? Sure! "The cigarette you truly enjoy," Dr. Almayrac has pointed out, "does not hurt you."

But why do all the traditional programs warn against "having just one?" You have probably had the experience of quitting for a while and then, after "having just one," finding yourself soon back to your old level of smoking, maybe a pack or more a day. In most traditional stop-smoking programs, if you return to smoking—be it a single cigarette or a whole carton—this is naturally considered a failure, backsliding, losing ground. Suddenly, then, if you do not approach your lapse with joy, not only do you not enjoy the cigarette you decided to smoke, you do not enjoy yourself at all. You do not enjoy the whole stop-smoking process. And you do not enjoy your past, your present, or your future. And as we have already pointed out, it's this "not enjoying yourself" that weakens you, robs you of your true energy, your power to go where you want to go in your life.

The reason having "just one" is so dangerous is not because of the cigarette itself but because it is very difficult to smoke and still enjoy all your thoughts about yourself.

So if you have just one (or two, or three—sometimes they go so quickly you've had three before you know it!), your challenge is to return to your joy as quickly as you can. Chances are that, for one reason or another, you were not enjoying yourself when you decided to have a smoke.

What's the best thing to do, the most efficient thing to do, when you have forgotten to enjoy yourself? Right! Enjoy the fact that you forgot to enjoy yourself! That's the quickest way to return to your happiness!

What if you are feeling guilty about smoking one or two or three? What do you do? Right! Enjoy yourself feeling guilty!

What if you are frightened that you will fail again in your efforts? What do you do? Right! Enjoy your fear, enjoy your uncertainty.

Returning to your own innate happiness, your inner joy, is always the primary and empowering strategy of the enlightened approach. No matter where you are on the map—you can always return to your joy, your inner happiness. Your inner happiness never leaves you. You can cover it up, push it down, smother it with your cultural conditioning, but it is an aspect of your own spirit and thus is never absent from where you are.

If you honestly smoke a cigarette and enjoy yourself—before, during, and after—then having a cigarette does not hurt you, does not deny the "smokeless" direction you have decided to follow in your life. It's not the cigarette—the reintroduction of nicotine—

that brings you down, that brings a halt to the whole stop-smoking process, but rather the thoughts you have about yourself for doing it.

In Chapter 1, we referred to the Gallup poll sponsored by *American Health* magazine and Campbell's Soup Company, which determined that more people change their lives and their lifestyles when they are feeling good about themselves and want to feel still better, than they do because of either social pressure or health concerns. The reason having one cigarette is dangerous is because it offers a huge temptation for you to think poorly of yourself. And when you think poorly of yourself, you don't have the energy to continue with the changes you have determined to make.

The reason you find yourself with a cigarette, after you have determined you won't smoke again, is generally because you are reacting to that old, tired, familiar recurring thought, "I want a cigarette—I need a cigarette." Consciously or subconsciously, you think that the only way you can get rid of that incessant thought is by having a cigarette. But if you pause and enjoy a minute or two, you'll realize this is not the case. We've already shown how you can enjoy the thought of smoking without actually acting on it. You can enjoy it just as it is, or you are free to change it: "I need a big, six-foot-long cigarette," or "I need a teeny, tiny little toothpick of a cigarette," or you can make the thought appear in big bold letters or in skywriting. You can move the thought into your little toe—try thinking it from there! You are free to play with all of your thoughts until you enjoy them, including the thought, "I need a cigarette." When you enjoy your thoughts, they no longer have command power.

In more traditional (less enlightened!) programs, you are not supposed to have, let alone enjoy, the thought, "I need a cigarette."

So many smokers assume that if the thought arises, it's a sign that they, personally, aren't ready, that they haven't done their homework, that they are weak, still addicted, still bound. As we know, however, the mere occurrence of the thought does not indicate that you need to act on it. Still, you also know from long experience that if you do act on that forbidden thought by simply smoking a cigarette, it will leave you alone, at least for a while. And, in the past, that's exactly how you have found relief from that thought.

It is this single thought—I need a cigarette—that smokers are trying to relieve or escape from when they smoke a cigarette. But the thought keeps coming back, hour after hour, day after day, month after month, year after year. To get out of the loop, to break the vicious cycle, you simply have to change your *response* to this single thought.

INSIGHT

You don't have to change the thought itself. You just have to change your response *to it.*

In the enlightened approach, you have learned to *love* all thoughts and that thought in particular. *Enjoy* that thought, play with it, dance with it, make it large then small, fat then skinny; have so much fun with it that it is completely *smothered* in happiness, in joy. In this way, it is finally dissolved, spent, at rest.

Until this enlightened approach was made clear, you've probably hated the thought, either consciously or subconsciously, for so long that it may take a day, a week, or a month to learn how to accept and enjoy it. But once you make peace with the thought and learn to enjoy it enough that you aren't always trying to make it go away, then it need never again return to you with any brittleness, pain or pushy demands. Sure, it may visit you again, weeks, months, or even years later, but it will do so playfully, easily. And you will discover that the thought—I want a cigarette—will dissolve gently, easily. Never again will you be truly motivated to act out the thought. You will simply play with it and enjoy it.

As you practice enjoying all of your thoughts, you'll discover it's easier to for you enjoy this particular one. As you practice choosing your thoughts, playing with your thoughts—dropping the ones you don't enjoy, bringing back the ones you do—you'll discover it's very easy to do the same thing with your smoking thoughts. When you have no thoughts about smoking that bother you, then you're free!

So, with the enlightened approach, you are free to smoke or not to smoke, as long as you enjoy all of your thoughts while doing so. You will discover that this freedom to smoke takes away much of the pressure. You will also discover that your desire to smoke diminishes in direct relation to the amount of *joy* you allow yourself in everything else that you do.

Professional Resistance

As you might expect, we've had health professionals (most of whom have never smoked) deny the validity of giving smokers this freedom and the efficacy of such a strategy. The professionals believe that, given the freedom to smoke, smokers won't try hard enough to refrain. Smokers will refuse to suffer for long periods of time and will refuse to give it their total blood-and-guts effort.

And we quickly agree, quickly confess: Smokers who employ the enlightened approach *don't* give themselves a hard time. They *don't* put themselves through blood-and-guts trials. They *don't* put themselves through mental and emotional anguish. Consequently, we have a very high success rate with smokers who follow this path. For most smokers, the enlightened approach is a wonderful, life-saving strategy that rings deeply true to them and thus helps them immediately to move out of the smoking loop.

Quitting smoking is very much like a love relationship. If you chase too hard, too fast, the chase is often unsuccessful. Or, if it is successful after such a fast and furious chase, it doesn't last. Balance is necessary. And your own inner happiness is the great balancer, the great equalizer, the life fulcrum on which you can place your trust.

You grow into freedom from smoking, just as you grow into love. At some point you make a commitment. You say "Yes. This is it. From here on, I devote my life to something [someone] new." But you do so out of joy, out of a growing sense of the amazing wonder that has come into your life. And just like falling in love, when you find freedom from smoking you become some-one completely new, yet someone closer to your true self than you've ever been.

Who is your true self? For that, of course, we need a whole new chapter.

17 What Is Your Original Face?
Who Will You Be Without Your Smokes?

> When Ming the monk overtook the fugitive Hui-neng, he wanted
> Hui-neng to give up the secret of Zen [happiness]. Hui-neng
> replied, "What are your original features which you have even
> prior to your birth?"
> —D. T. Suzuki

Who Are You Going to Be After You Quit?

Smoking is a kid's attraction that leads to adult entrapment.
Surveys show that more than eighty percent of long-term smokers begin smoking before the age of eighteen years, and forty percent of these begin at age of fourteen or younger. If you didn't
start smoking before age eighteen, it is likely that you did start
smoking by age twenty-one. This means that in all likelihood you
probably don't know what it's like to be an adult and a nonsmoker.
But don't let that frighten you. This is one more area where practicing the Enlightenment Exercise brings back your sense of
adventure.

In the Zen tradition, enlightenment, or *satori,* is considered
to be your original condition. Enlightenment is not something you
add on or develop; rather, it is a quality of consciousness that is
ever-present, but one that you discover or recognize through various disciplines and teachings.

Likewise, the person you are without cigarettes is not someone totally new and different, but someone who was there all along, whom you discover anew through various disciplines and teachings.

High School Reunion?

You've probably had the experience of spending some time with a friend or group of friends (or even relatives!), whom you haven't seen in ten, fifteen, or twenty years. In such a situation, you generally laugh a lot when you first get together, thrilled with the mutual task of "shrinking the decades" and catching up on all that's gone on in your lives: the marriages and divorces, births and deaths, new jobs and old jobs. Such reacquainting is one of the pleasures of growing older.

But, after you have shrunk the years, isn't it interesting to discover this *new* person who is standing before you? Someone whose politics, or religion, or personal life, or financial condition, or traveling experience makes them different from the person you remember. At the same time, though, these differences somehow accentuate the person who was there all along.

In other words, for most of us, when we do it right, the years work to bring out who we truly are. Our experiences function to bring us closer to ourselves, such that we are able to express not so much the schooling or culture or times that surround us but more of the truth of who and what we are inside. Growing older, we grow into our truer, deeper selves.

Moving into your nonsmoking self is in fact moving closer to who you really are—not who you were prior to smoking. (You won't go back to being a teenager again—thank God!). Rather, you become who you have been growing toward in your maturity. Dropping smoking is simply dropping one more persona that no longer suits you. It may have suited you once, a long time ago— just as the persona of the high school cheerleader, or the football star, or of the kid in the corner suited you. But with age and experience such a persona no longer suits you; you realize it's time to move on. Who you truly are, who you have been all along but were unable to express, is now emerging.

So who is this new/old person, this nonsmoker who is emerging?

D. T. Suzuki, who many consider to be the "Father of Zen in the West" because of his many translations as well as original works on Zen, wrote:

The worst enemy of Zen experience, at least in the beginning, is the intellect, which consists and insists in discriminating subject from object. The discriminating intellect, therefore, must be cut short if Zen consciousness is to unfold itself."

If the joyful consciousness is to unfold itself within you, the strictly analytical, divisive use of your mind must be allowed to rest as you let your inner joy find its way to the surface.

Childlike Trust

Whosoever shall not receive the kingdom of God [enlightenment] as a little child, he shall not enter therein.
—Mark 10.15

You need not figure out who you are or who you will be without cigarettes, any more than a grade-school child needs to figure out who he or she is on the playground. You need simply to enjoy who you are—enjoy all the different feelings, impulses, directions, and diversions that come your way.

When you first started smoking, you didn't necessarily try to figure out who you would be—what kind of a smoker, or what kind of a person you would be. You may have had some role models and some ideals (Ahh, youth!), but you just moved ahead into that new identity. It was a new adventure, a new world that you were ready to explore.

The same is true when you move away from smoking. You may have an ideal, a role model, but basically you create it, you experience it, you enjoy it as you go along. That's all you need to do.

Expect Surprises!

Being a nonsmoker is going to be different, actually much more pleasant and ordinary than you, as a smoker, might expect it to be.

One thing that almost every smoker experiences when quitting is just how commonplace, how ordinary nonsmoking appears to those around them. As a smoker, suddenly not smoking seems to be one of the most miraculous, strange, and unprecedented events in the world! After ten, twenty, or thirty or more years of smoking, to go one day, or one week, or one month without smoking seems to call for a ticker-tape parade and brass bands. Yet, many smokers have related that even their *spouses* failed to notice their nonsmoking! "From my perspective," one housewife reported to me, "it was as if I just had my legs chopped off, my face removed, and my sex changed, but nobody seemed to notice."

Another phenomenon most smokers find surprising is just how *peaceful* not smoking is. From the smoker's perspective, quitting smoking is traditionally viewed as warfare: daily battles with powerful foes that leave no moment unscathed. When the experience of not smoking turns out to be quiet, tranquil, and relaxed, many smokers become concerned: "How can it be so peaceful?" they wonder.

What smokers discover is the tranquility and peace they have developed over the years, but which they have generally ignored or covered up with their intellect and daily habit of struggle. Happiness is the sign (and the origin!) of a peaceful consciousness!

Not Smoking Is a By-Product of the New You!

As we've stressed from the beginning of this book, your stopping smoking is not the primary goal of this process. The primary goal is to help you enjoy yourself more. Who you enjoy is not a different person than you are now. When you begin enjoying your thoughts, that enlightened persona you had before you were born begins to shine through. The spirit of your individual being comes to the fore. You enjoy yourself more than you ever dreamed possible.

This brighter, happier, more genuine self is the self you have always been, the self you always knew was in there, potentiated, wanting to come out. Now you know how to set the deeper, truer self loose: Simply practice the Enlightenment Exercise!

The natural result of this emerging self is the falling away of those habits and activities that no longer serve your purposes. The cocoon is necessary for the emerging butterfly; the eggshell is necessary for the emerging eagle; your "old self" is necessary for what is yet to come. But then the cocoon, the eggshell, your old self all fall away as the more powerful, more beautiful, and freer being emerges.

Enjoy the new you that is coming through! You need not figure out who you are supposed to be, who you might be, or who you should be. Just enjoy yourself each moment—be who you are in each moment—and those questions will be answered perfectly, every day, every year. You are an enlightened being. You enlighten others. Enjoy!

In the next chapter we will take a look at one aspect of the "new you"—the one person many smokers *least* want to meet, because this is the person who is tempted to exchange food for tobacco. Chapter 18 gives you something sweet and nourishing to chew on.

18 The Sound of One Hand Eating

I Have to Smoke or I'll Get Fat!

> When you are at table—think of the heavenly table, of the food that is served thereon, which food is God Himself [Bliss], and of the guests at this table, who are the angels.
> —St. Teresa of Avila

Donna, a pretty woman in her early thirties, was dragged by her girlfriend to the first class of one of my "How to Forget to Smoke" programs. Donna appeared to be maybe fifteen or twenty pounds overweight (from the perspective of our current "Twiggy" culture standards). Throughout that first class, Donna sat silent with her arms folded across her chest, apparently daring me to convince her to enjoy her happiness. By the end of the evening, she did loosen up a bit, even laughed a couple of times, but still she wasn't having any of this quitting smoking business. She wasn't coming back to the second class. She didn't want to risk the possibility that she might accidentally quit, or even, as the class title suggested was possible, forget to smoke.

"I have to smoke," she said. "Otherwise, I'd gain so much weight I couldn't live with myself."

I suggested that, smoking or not smoking, she didn't need to gain weight if she wasn't happy to do so.

"Everybody gains weight when they quit," she said. "That's a proven fact."

"My sister just quit after smoking thirty years," a man piped in, "and she didn't gain an ounce."

"Well," Donna said. "That's hard for me to believe, because studies have shown...."

Donna held fast to her position. For her, it obviously was not the right time to quit, under those circumstances, with those beliefs, because surely she would gain weight if she believed she would, and for her, apparently, that was a fate worse than death.

We wished her the best and enjoyed her for being honest and up front about her feelings. (We never try to convert somebody to our way of thinking. We only share what we've learned, by talking and by demonstration, and then, as best we can, enjoy the response. The law by which we apply the Law of Happiness is: Do unto others as you would have them do unto you.) It was clear to me, though I didn't say so at the time, that the weight of Donna's heavy thoughts was already showing itself in her life and would continue to do so, whether she smoked or didn't smoke.

Too often as we eat, we take in food with one hand and shove it away with another (mental) hand, when we think "I shouldn't eat this." This heavy mental battle makes us flabby, but we assume we have to participate in the battle, because it has its roots in scientific studies. If we live our lives according to what "scientific studies have shown," rather than according to what we are personally happy thinking contrary to current cultural conditioning, we're going to be in big trouble! Here's why.

The Latest Research About Food: Don't Eat It!

A number of the latest studies suggest, basically, that food is not good for you. That's right! As the inspirational author Hugh

Prather has pointed out, except for brussels sprouts and okra, we now have scientific studies that show just about anything else you eat has, from some scientist's point of view, some type of deleterious effect.

For instance, some studies suggest you should not eat any kind of meat whatsoever. Other researchers suggest that a vegetarian diet is not "natural" for the human system and lacks sufficient protein, which one study says you need lots of, and another study says you need hardly any of. One study says too many carbohydrates make you hungry. Another study indicates that dairy is not good for you. Still other studies say that absolutely none of the grains is truly compatible with the human digestive system. Some studies say you shouldn't eat chickens or eggs grown in commercial operations. Others say the pesticides on our fruit are so bad that you shouldn't eat commercially grown fruit. And of course, stay away from coffee, strong tea, sweet drinks, and carbonated drinks. Also, bottled water is not all that it's made out to be. Finally, any kind of alcohol is a "no no," unless it's red wine, and then . . . well, different studies conclude different things.

It seems that whatever we eat or drink, we aren't supposed to eat or drink. Celery and carrot sticks may be all right for a while, but make sure they're organically grown. WARNING: You can literally starve to death on a diet of celery—one study found that it takes more calories to eat celery than are contained in celery. And wasn't there a study recently about the bad effects of beta-carotene? And don't carrots have sugar? You'd better go easy on the carrot sticks, too.

That's only the food itself. We are also warned about its preparation. One study warns against lightly cooked food, as "light cooking" does not destroy all harmful bacteria. Another study warns against cooking food too much, as it depletes some of the nutrients and can produce carcinogens. One group recommends *never* microwaving anything. Another group says not to use the barbecue. One group says eat only raw, organically grown vegetables and fruits, but not too many!

When should you eat? Never in the heat of the day, never one hour before swimming, never between meals, never after 6 P.M., never when you are in a hurry, never when you aren't feeling well.

What about combinations of foods? Don't eat meat with potatoes, fruit with salad, hot with cold, or dessert with anything!

On and on it goes. With all of this "scientific information" about all various aspects of eating coming our way day after day—supposedly for our own good—is it any wonder that so many adults have food problems? Food problems that we unknowingly pass on to our kids, and food problems that we, in our time, unknowingly received from our parents.

There is good news, however. All of the studies agree that the food you eat will either make you healthy and thin or make you sick and fat. The bad news is that none of the studies agrees as to which foods do what.

More promising studies indicate that centenarians—those who have lived to be one hundred years old or more—share no common dietary habits! Some of them eat meat, some don't. Some drink alcohol, some don't. Some eat one meal a day. Some eat four meals a day. One thing they all do have in common, however, is a lighthearted, easy-going approach to life. They practice the *Enlightenment Exercise!*

After all, it is "Not that which goeth into the mouth defileth a man; but that which cometh out of the mouth, this defileth a man" (Matthew 15.11).

It is a brave discipline in this age of ours to eat and not think in a negative manner about what you are eating, how you are eating, when you are eating. Simply to eat *what* you want, *when* you want it, and then to go on about your business, without condemning or congratulating yourself, is the most healthful dietary discipline you can follow.

When you stop smoking, you may discover that food starts tasting better than it has in years! That's a withdrawal you can enjoy, yes? You don't need to make it into a problem. You may also find yourself wanting to eat to replace the oral stimulation that smoking provided. Okay. Do it! Enjoy it! Only when you do not enjoy your thoughts or your food while eating will you have an eating problem. And then, the problem isn't really your eating, is it? Right. It's your level of joy.

Deepak Chopra tells the story of a research project in which rabbits were being fed a diet that the researchers assumed would lead to very high cholesterol. Sure enough, after the allotted time all the rabbits were showing very high cholesterol levels, except for one group, whose cholesterol remained normal. The researchers could not understand why this batch was not affected—the living conditions were the same, the heavy fat diet was the same, and the feeding schedule was the same. Finally, they discovered that the lab assistant who had fed that particular group of rabbits had consistently picked up, hugged, and fondled the rabbits, and cooed over them prior to their feeding. In such a state of love, the poisonous diet was poisonous no more!

Sondra Ray, in her delightful little book, *The Only Diet There Is,* writes:

It is not what you eat that can hurt you. It is what you BELIEVE about what you eat that can hurt you.... Therefore, food is not "fattening" by itself. The thoughts you have about food are what make it fattening.... A study done on people weighing precisely their desired weight showed that all of them could eat anything they wanted without any concern or worry.... They could do so because all of them had one thing in common. They all had the thought that they could eat whatever and whenever they wanted without gaining weight. "I never gain weight" is simple enough.... Your body always obeys the instructions of your mind. It is the instructions you give your body about food that matter.... Attitude and belief are the common denominators of all the causes of obesity.... What causes you to be overweight is what you believe.... The cause that never fails to produce results all the time is thought.

She concludes by suggesting, "our true nourishment comes to us from the light of God, not from food."

Therese Neumann, the Catholic saint of Bavaria, demonstrated the nourishment from the light of God—the power of truly enlightened living—for over twenty years.

During her fast since 1927, [Therese Neumann] has not eaten even one meal a day. She has not eaten even one small piece of bread once a day, once a week, once a month, or once a year. She has not drunk even a teaspoonful of water, coffee, tea, wine, milk, or medicine once a day, once a week, once a month, or once a year. In September 1947, it was twenty years since any natural nourishment of any kind passed [her] lips, and for years before 1927 she had eaten very little food and taken almost nothing to drink.

And we're worried that enlightenment won't be powerful enough to help us keep off a few pounds after quitting?

How Not to Gain Weight After Quitting

We stop having food and weight issues when we are able to enjoy all of our thoughts about eating and not eating! In the same way that we heal our past by thinking thoughts we enjoy in the moment, every moment, so too do we heal our future by thinking thoughts we enjoy right now.

So start right now by not setting yourself up to gain weight. If you think, "It's going to be tough to not to gain weight when I quit smoking," then sure enough, it's going to be tough. On the other hand, if you think, "This way of quitting allows me to quit without gaining any weight," then sure enough, you'll be able to quit and not gain weight.

Again, and still, your *joy* is the key. As you enjoy yourself more, enjoy your thoughts and feelings, your relationships, your daily experiences, you won't look to food as your source of happiness. And, as an added benefit, you'll discover that you enjoy food more than ever! Sometimes you'll eat a lot of it. Other times you'll forget to eat any of it. Both ways are perfect!

When you practice the Enlightenment Exercise in regard to your food, you'll find that you give yourself permission to take time to prepare the meals you love. You'll give yourself time to sit and eat with great freedom, lack of guilt, easy companionship.

If, like most of us in the contemporary world, you do indeed have food issues that have been with you for many years, then you will find it very helpful to do some journal-writing about your food thoughts just as you wrote in your journal about your smoking thoughts.

Remember the Law of Happiness: *Enjoying your life is the most important thing for you and for everybody around you*. So enjoying your food is important not only for you but for all those around you. And the only way you can enjoy your food is to enjoy your thoughts about your food: about the food you are eating, about the food you just ate, and about the food you are going to eat. *All* of your thoughts about food need to be enjoyed. When you have succeeded in this great discipline, you will discover that you always eat just the right amount at the right time to satisfy and delight you.

Exercise

Write in your journal, "I eat all I want and never gain weight." What thoughts come up? Write them down. Keep writing, "I eat all I want and never gain weight" until all the thoughts that come up are thoughts you enjoy.

Write in your journal, "Stopping smoking doesn't mean gaining weight." What thoughts come up? Write them down. Play with these thoughts until you are happy with all of them!

So the secret to mastering food is to love it and not be afraid of it or make it into more than it is. In the next chapter, we will see that this, in fact, is the secret to mastering every aspect of tobacco addiction and devotion.

19 You Can't Master What You Don't Love

How and Why to Love All Your Fellow Smokers, All Those Ex-Smokers, and Especially All the Anti-Smokers

> Forgive us our trespasses [unhappinesses] as we forgive those who trespass against us.
> —from The Lord's Prayer

Do you ever wonder what's the greatest thing you could wish for when you wish upon a star? Or, what's the best wish to wish when you're about to blow out your birthday candles? That is, other than for a new car or new lover or a great pair of socks? How about this? "No matter how many souls there are in the universe, may they all be enlightened!"

In the Buddhist tradition, this is what is known as the *bodhisattva vow,* which is an attitude taken by those who have already attained a certain degree of enlightenment. A bodhisattva determines to stay "in form"—that is, to stay in the world—with all the other beings. Rather than dissolving into the Infinite Unformed Happiness, he or she vows to stay in form until all beings have likewise learned to transcend all form and similarly can dissolve in bliss.

In some ways the bodhisattva vow is a quieter, more inward expression of the same motivation that Christian missionaries have shown over the millennia. When you have something good, there's a natural urge to want to share it with everyone. This urge is a sign of our deeper knowledge that we are all one.

The Smoking Bodhisattva?

In an earlier chapter, we alluded to the fact that your personal experience with smoking and finding freedom from addiction will prove helpful to others, either directly or indirectly. The reverse is also true: As you help other smokers, you discover your own energies are purified, clarified, intensified.

So how do you help others? Don't worry. You don't have to go knocking on their doors! As you might suspect, having read this far, the best way you can help others, at least in the beginning, is to clear your own mind about their smoking and not smoking and anti-smoking. How do you clear your mind? By enjoying them and their smoking, and their not smoking and their anti-smoking. Your joy is indeed the most important thing for you and for them—it is a valuable, highly contagious energy.

So let's begin with your relations with other smokers. In the same way that you have learned to be free of thoughts you do not enjoy about your own smoking behavior, you can "practice" by dropping, changing, or rearranging thoughts you don't enjoy about other smoking behaviors.

Almost every smoker feels he or she knows the "right way" and the wrong way to smoke. Most smokers assume that they know the right time, the right place, the right brand, the right way to hold the cigarette, and the right way to inhale, exhale, and generally be *cool* about the whole affair. You've probably felt this way yourself. And you're right—you do know all these things. We are happy to recognize that every smoker is smoking just the way he or she thinks is best. How fun! How crazy! How true!

The goal here, then, is consciously to give credit to other smokers for smoking perfectly! Or more precisely, to start enjoying other smokers for believing they are smoking perfectly. Don't judge them harshly. Be on their side. Be their friend. Enjoy them just as they are.

You don't have to go knocking on their doors to do this. They don't even need to know you are enjoying them and their smoking rituals. In fact, most will never know, consciously, what you are doing.

As you learn to enjoy all of your smoking friends and even smoking strangers, you'll discover it's easier to enjoy your own behaviors. When you give up judging the good or bad way that others smoke, you give yourself more room to be yourself.

What about the twelve-year-old smoker? Or the ten-year-old smoker? Are you just going to enjoy their smoking and their silly ways? Yes. Them most especially!

It doesn't mean you have to be quiet about it, or that you can't step in and say what's appropriate for the moment. But the ten-year-old or the twelve-year-old smoker is going to be much more open to you, much more willing to listen to you, to be influenced by you, if you are enjoying them in that moment, loving them, being with them, understanding them, rather than condemning and berating them. Your joy is always the most important thing for you and for everybody around you!

As you practice enjoying other smokers, one or two at a time, you will help to dissolve the cloud of heavy condemnation that surrounds all smokers. And in this way you will help yourself.

What About Ex-Smokers?

Every smoker has encountered the ex-smoker who says something like, "I just decided to quit, so I did it. Nothing to it, really. You could, too, if you really wanted to." They say it in such a way that it makes you want to pinch their nose.

Other ex-smokers might say something like, "Quitting smoking was the worst thing I ever went through. It was horrible. Still is, sometimes. I sometimes wonder if it was worth it!" Of course, this gives you much encouragement.

Again, the work here is to enjoy if not the ex-smokers themselves then at least your reaction to them. You don't have to worry about them. You only have to deal with how their words or attitudes make you feel inside. You need to play the Enlightenment Game with them, too, so that you enjoy everything and everyone connected with smoking. The only way you can accomplish that is to enjoy your thoughts.

If you don't enjoy your thoughts automatically, you may want to play the "reframing game" with what ex-smokers tell you. For instance, you might want to exaggerate their words, either silently or to them, depending on how you're feeling. "Oh, so it was easy? Like eating ice cream, would you say? Or like falling on the ice?" Or, "You say it was horrible? Where exactly was it horrible? Was it horrible in your nose or in your ears or in your brain? Which part of your brain was it horrible in?"

Again, the intent here is to do whatever it takes to *enjoy* yourself with ex-smokers. Enjoy your response to them. Enjoy the fact that they did it, however they did it, knowing you will do it, too, in the only way you can do it. Most ex-smokers will be easy to enjoy—

they will be compassionate, and supportive, and very understanding. Let them be! Give yourself permission to enjoy them and not be defensive with them. Let them be your friends and confidants. Enjoy the whole process.

As you enjoy ex-smokers more, your chances of becoming an ex-smoker and staying an ex-smoker naturally increase. And your joy helps build a path for other smokers to enjoy ex-smokers. This is a bodhisattva work!

What About The Anti-Smokers?

"No tobacco has ever touched these lips. These lips are too pure for such defilement." You've heard it before, if not in these exact words, then at least with this same attitude. This is the smoker's greatest challenge: the person who has never smoked and is offended by all who do.

Again, the work here is to learn to enjoy your reactions to these affronts. You don't have to learn to enjoy or even accept such people's views of smoking and smokers. When it comes to tobacco, you are the expert. You know better than to toss the personal lives, personal pleasures, of millions of people onto the trash heap. You know all the trails you have walked to get to where you are, and there's no reason to defile these memories.

So if you find yourself irritated with such self-righteousness, enjoy your irritation. If you find yourself combative, enjoy your combativeness. If you find yourself shrinking away, enjoy shrinking away. You are training yourself to master the whole of the tobacco experience and that means you are learning to love (to enjoy!) the whole world of tobacco—the smokers, ex-smokers, anti-smokers, nonsmokers, growers, distributors, and advertisers. Why not? It's your world!

When you are enjoying yourself, and your reactions, you are able to communicate with others more freely, more openly, and others are more anxious to hear what you have to say. As a smoker or ex-smoker in the contemporary world, you can't help but run into the antismoking "no-never-not-me!" people. Part of your work is to bring them enlightenment, and the only way you can bring them enlightenment is to enjoy yourself in their company. As you enjoy yourself in their company, you will spontaneously say and do the right thing—or maybe spontaneously *not* say or do something. Joy is the key. Joy is your protector and guide and "escape vehicle." And joy is what will help bring an end to the tobacco wars.

Forgive the Tobacco Companies!

Are the tobacco companies to blame for your unhappiness? To some extent, certainly they are. The tobacco companies chose to put higher levels of nicotine in your smokes. They chose to make smoking attractive to you when you were a kid. They consciously withheld information from you that, if you had known it, might have made you think twice about starting or continuing to smoke. (Because we know—don't we?—that information is all it takes for you to decide to smoke or not to smoke!)

Not to blame the tobacco companies is a brave and rare attitude for smokers, ex-smokers, and anti-smokers in this day and age, but it is the most healthy attitude you can take. Why hold the grudge? You were grateful for the many years tobacco companies worked to make tobacco available to you, day after day, year after year, from a thousand different outlets. They made different brands available, different sizes, different strengths. So now they're the bad guys?

One of our hopes for this book is that it will eliminate the adverse attitude about tobacco. After all, when you take away the good guys and bad guys, you are left with the truth, and the truth sets you free. Sure, you can make a great case, if that's your inclination. But to what end? Are you going to try to collect from the tobacco companies all the money you spent on health bills, etc.? To do that, you're going to have to get really sick and then you're going to have to prove that tobacco is what made you sick, or is about to kill you!

That's a battle that, even if you win, you lose.

If you want to get healthy, you have to throw such proof out the window, don't you? If you want to guard against cancer, emphysema, heart disease, and other health problems, you have to start clearing out all the things that are eating at you, all the things that are clogging your joy and slowing your happiness. What good does it do to fight the tobacco companies?

Don't worry—we have plenty of fighters out there who are more than willing to carry on that battle. You don't need to. You can get free of the tobacco wars just by deciding that you are not going to be angry or unhappy at anybody for any reason, because you know that your life is too precious, too beautiful, too holy to defile it in that way.

And what about those who are working for the tobacco companies? My suggestion to you is to find a different job. It's the same suggestion I make to those who are in the military: Find a different job. The times are not right for such vocations. The times are such that we are working to bring each other enlightenment, peace, prosperity. The old ways no longer work. Find a different way to do it. Tobacco has proven to be an inefficient way to bring pleasure to the masses. Find a different job. You don't want to be put in a position where you have to lie or be somber all the time. You want to enjoy your work—your *daily occupation.* If you work for the tobacco companies, find a different job. If you grow tobacco, find a different crop. Even making such a suggestion, I am happy for what has been! I have no war to wage against our history, but I am ready to help make a brighter future, a wider peace.

When we release our anger, fear, and frustration with all the other players in the tobacco wars and the tobacco games, we are free of their hold on us. As Emmet Fox wrote in *The Power of Constructive Thinking:*

Resentment is really a form of attachment. It is a cosmic truth that it takes two to make a prisoner; the prisoner and the jailer. . . . When you hold resentment against anyone, you are bound to that person by a cosmic link, a real, though mental chain. You are tied by a cosmic tie to the thing that you hate. . . . The object of your resentment will be drawn again into your life, perhaps to work further havoc. Do you think you can afford this?

It is possible to be free not only of the tobacco habit, but also of the negative physical and mental residue left by the habit. Giving up the war against the tobacco companies is a big step in gaining freedom from all the negative effects of tobacco.

Universalize Your Exercise!

As you recognize that enjoying happiness is the most important thing for *other* people and for everyone around other people, you begin to deepen and broaden your own joy. As you direct your attention toward recognizing the presence of other people's joy, your own joy naturally expands.

Likewise, as you do your "inner work," the preparatory work of learning to enjoy your smoking and your not smoking, and learning to enjoy other people's smoking, not smoking, and anti-smoking and pro-smoking, you become more free to do what you most want to do.

So in the enlightened approach to quitting smoking, you discover that you are indeed acting as a bodhisattva—in this case, a smoker who, in finding your own freedom, helps find freedom for the whole. By now you can see how the whole process works. It is a lot easier, more enjoyable, and more immediate than it might have appeared at the beginning of Chapter 1. Enlightenment is always easier, more enjoyable, and more immediate than it might appear at first!

———

Exercise

Practice thinking of yourself as enlightened—as someone who knows how to love and be happy, how to be Christlike or Buddhalike all of the time, no matter what the world is doing.

You don't need to be gleeful or smug. Just be who you are—deeply who you are. Enjoy one day after another. If you are still a smoker, be an enlightened smoker. If you are finally an ex-smoker, be an enlightened ex-smoker. The world needs you in this mode!

It is alright to be enlightened. As you train yourself to enjoy your thoughts—all the time, every day, everywhere—you are taking up the ancient enlightenment discipline. "How beautiful upon the mountains are the feet of him that bringeth good [joyful] tidings, that publisheth peace [happiness]" (Isaiah 52.7).

The next chapter brings us full circle and we can look back at the steps we have taken so far, and ahead to the new territory unfolding before us. It has been easy, hasn't it?

20 The No-Fault Divorce

So Long Tobacco, It's Been Good to Know You. . . . Hello, Freedom, It's Good to Meet You!

> I find the great thing in the world is not so much where we stand [in relation to happiness] as what direction we are moving.
> —Johann Wolfgang von Goethe

Here we are at the start of the last chapter, and many readers have already quit smoking. Congratulations! We trust you are enjoying your newfound freedom! It will grow deeper, broader, and more enjoyable as the months and years proceed.

Other smokers are almost ready, having been faithfully practicing the enlightenment exercise, playing with their thoughts, their smokes, loosening up, definitely understanding the whole process. If this is how you are feeling, let me boldly suggest that you *are* close, you *are* ready to do it, and it *will* be easier than you ever imagined. Go for it! You'll soon see what a pleasure this enlightened quitting can be!

And finally, of course, others are happy just reading, hanging out. That's perfect. You've been doing what you were asked to do.

If this is where you are, you may be wondering, "Is that all there is? Isn't there some more involved secret? Some final magical fireworks to set off that will explode my brain and make the tobacco habit fall away, leaving me happy and free?" Indeed, there is! The involved secret and the magical fireworks are contained in two words: *more practice.*

Rudolph Steiner, a clairvoyant whose work in the early part of the 1900s influenced the direction of a dozen different professional disciplines, wrote:

Students lose courage because they consider their first experiences worthless or because these experiences seem insignificant and unlikely to lead to anything more valuable in the foreseeable future. . . . *We must eradicate the belief that only bizarre and mysterious practices lead to higher knowledge.* We should be clear that development begins with the feelings and thoughts we live with all the time, but that these feelings and thoughts must be given a new, unaccustomed direction (emphasis added).

So your first "assignment" as you begin this last chapter of the book is to enjoy your feelings—whatever they might be. If you are excited about the possibilities that have been discussed up to this point, enjoy being excited. If you are worried, enjoy being worried. If you are disappointed, enjoy being disappointed. Your willingness to enjoy being where you are right now, feeling what you feel right now, will lead you to the exact right "next use" of this book!

A Step-by-Step Review

Let's quickly review the seven steps.

In Step One, of course, you simply read the book, doing nothing more than hanging out, doing *satsang* (i.e., being in the company of truth). You might feel like doing Step One all over again. Just read the book again, hang out some more. That's fine! you might be surprised what new things catch your eye on a second or third reading. Each time you read the book, you are taking another step toward quitting. Do this first step as many times as you are happy to do it. You are perfectly free to do it that way! And it *will* help dissolve your tobacco habit.

Be (happily!) forewarned: Just hanging out, thinking about what is being said, undoubtedly has already had some effect on your smoking, be it slight or significant. When I suggested, early on, that you have a right and even a spiritual obligation to enjoy smoking, you immediately began to view your smoking from a wider, freer perspective (even if you didn't then realize it). The work has already begun, even if you're still in Step One. Take it as many times as you want—it works!

In Step Two, you begin studying, contemplating, digging deeper into the material. The best way to do this is to begin playing with your thoughts, all day, every day, so that you enjoy more of them more often than you have ever done in the past. That's the true *study* suggested here—the study of your ability to enjoy your happiness. When you enjoy your thoughts, you make a connection with the Christ, the *atman* (the eternal within), the Buddha nature. Such a connection cannot help but speed the evolution of good things into your life.

You might also begin Step Two—studying more intensely— by accepting the possibility that your smoking has been a spiritual quest and thus a spiritual discipline. It's an unusual view, but one that leads you to a much larger framework in which to view the smoking process. Start exploring other spiritual disciplines. Look up the references found in this book—check out the original material. You will discover that the Great Tradition of spiritual teachings and teachers is alive and well today (more so than any other time in history!) and offers much to make your daily life—whether urban or suburban—a consistently delightful experience. Determine to study the disciplines and teachings to which your joy is drawn. Your joy will lead you—as it has with this work—to the right books, the right teachers, the right programs and disciplines. Joy is your teacher and is an easy taskmaster.

In Step Three, you actually *do* the exercises suggested in this book. Some readers do the exercises as soon as they are offered, eager to relieve themselves of the tobacco habit as soon as possible, immediately confident in the wisdom of this enlightened approach. Other readers take it more slowly, doing some of the exercises, letting others wait until later. Still other readers skip all of the exercises—even the basic Enlightenment Exercise—curious to discover where the book is leading.

Whatever type of reader you were (are!), now is the time to go back and begin working through the exercises that most appealed to you, and to experiment with the ones that may have seemed strange or awkward. You can do them as they are offered, or you can let your inner happiness help you change them, rearrange them, or modify them, if that's what it takes to get started. As you actually begin doing the exercises—instead of just reading them or occasionally thinking about them—you will discover that your smoking life is indeed loosening up, the energies are starting to flow. These exercises act as joyful Drano for your clogged smoking pipes—your stopped-up emotions and backed-up habits.

In Step Four, you share this enlightenment adventure with other smokers. As we've said before, "If you want to learn something, teach it!" Chances are that unless you are reading this straight through in a cabin in the woods or have just moved to a new city and have no one at all to talk to, you've probably already shared at least an idea or two of this book informally, spontaneously, with someone else. That's natural. Let your joy unfold!

We want to nudge you now toward a more formal, or at least more concentrated sharing, simply because such sharing deepens the enlightenment message and grounds you in the work. When we teach people to lead classes in this method, we prepare them to allow the students to teach each other. This is not something we design into the class; rather, it's something we noticed happens time and time again. This phenomenon of students helping students always occurs, even if the instructor is an ex-smoker. It makes no difference that the instructor has been trained in this process and has memorized all of the exercises—that the vast enlightenment traditions are clearly focused in the instructor's mind. New students invariably take over class discussions, teaching each other with what they are learning. It somehow makes it more real, more tangible, more accessible, for *everybody,* when students share what they learn with each other.

The easiest way to share is simply to share this book with one or two of your smoking friends, if for no other reason than to hear their opinion of the enlightenment approach. You certainly don't need to be a missionary or a warrior for the cause. Simply share with an open (joyful!) attitude whatever their response might be.

When you have found one or two others who are attracted to the book, who like the approach, why not set out on the adventure together? Help each other to learn the Enlightenment Exercise. Practice the Enlightenment Exercise together. Help each other to think what you are most happy thinking about your smoking. Help each other find freedom!

Even if you don't find others to work with in this way, you can share the fundamental joy of life—enjoying your thoughts—with your family and friends, and, perhaps, with the person behind the cash register at the gas station, or the bus driver, or your fellow shopper. Enjoying your life is wonderful. Share it! You'll discover the world is a brighter place.

Step Five is the journal-writing process. If you haven't tried it yet, you're in for a sweet surprise. If you have tried it, you know how powerful it can be. The reason we have a two-thousand-year tradition of silent meditation and prayer—with hands folded and eyes closed, or led by someone in the front of the chapel/temple/synagogue—is because for two thousand years most of the world has not been able to read and write. Only in the last one hundred years or so has literacy started to make significant inroads. (Still, in 1997 only thirty percent of the world's population can read.) However, because *you* can read and write, you have access to a world of holy secrets that were reserved for the advanced priests and scribes in the ancient temples. The written prayer, the written meditation, is much more powerful than oral or silent prayer, in the same way that written goals and objectives are more powerful than goals and objectives that are only thought about. And, likewise, prayer and meditation are more powerful than the act of goal-setting. And finally, written prayer and meditation are much more powerful than written goal-setting.

Despite all this, this step seems to be one that many students are willing to skip, thinking it unnecessary for their progress. Because joy—happiness—is the only vital ingredient in this approach, journal-writing isn't strictly compulsory. Sure, you can walk behind the bullock cart, but your private jet awaits! The quickest, most efficient, most powerful way to access your joy, your inner happiness, is by writing your words, your thoughts on paper.

As you write words on paper, you bring your thoughts into the realm of the senses, visually and tactilely. This builds an invaluable bridge between your inner and outer joy.

More importantly, putting your words on paper helps you to see what you are thinking. Of course, you can and do see what you are thinking with your mind's eye, but when you put it on paper, you connect your inner eye with your outer eye. Such a link becomes the basis for spiritual development.

Dr. Ira Progoff, a psychotherapist who studied under two of the greatest minds of the East and West—C. G. Jung and D. T. Suzuki—conducted extensive research on life cycles in relation to spiritual and creative experience. From his research he created the intensive journal and journal feedback methods, which use journal-writing in therapeutic and spiritual balancing processes. His initial work with the many benefits of journal-writing helped form the basis for a wide variety of contemporary therapeutic and developmental disciplines that use the journal-writing process. The enlightened approach to journal-writing, as outlined in Chapter 3, is in our view a synthesis, a simplification, and an intensification of many of these modalities.

In Step Six, you create *rituals* with your daily smoking behavior. Obviously, many of the exercises given in this book encourage you to do just that. Make a ritual of your smoking? Why not? You'll enjoy it more than ever!

A Spiritual Aside

After completing the research and the writing of the first versions of this book, I happened on to the following short essay by Bhagwan Shree Rajneesh, the controversial "Rolls Royce Guru," who fell from grace, at least in the eyes of the U.S. Federal Government and many Western followers, when he was charged with tax evasion and false reporting of revenues and he quickly left the country.[*]

Rajneesh's advice to a thirty-year smoker is so similar (though not identical) to the strategy put forth in this book that it seems appropriate to include it here as an addendum in our last chapter.

Osho's Smoking Meditation

A man came to me. He had been suffering from chain-smoking for thirty years; he was ill, and the doctors said, "You will never be healthy if you don't stop smoking." But he was a chronic smoker; he could not help it. He had tried—not that he had not tried—he had tried hard, and he had suffered much in trying; but only for one day

---

[*] A spiritual teacher will not attract tens of thousands of followers—as Rajneesh did—if he does not offer them at least something that resonates deep within their hearts as being true. Earnest spiritual seekers continue on their upward paths, even if their teacher teeters or falls over a cliff. Such a fall does not reflect poorly on the seeker or the seeker's desire to reach the summit, or even necessarily on the path that the teacher revealed. Rajneesh changed his name to Osho, and his works continue to benefit many people.

or two days, and then again the urge would come so tremendously, it would simply take him away. Again he would fall into the same pattern.

Because of this smoking he had lost all self-confidence: he knew he could not do a small thing; he could not stop smoking. He had become worthless in his own eyes; he thought himself just the most worthless person in the world. He had no respect for himself. He came to me.

He said, "What can I do? How can I stop smoking?" I said, "Nobody can stop smoking. You have to understand. Smoking is not only a question of your decision now. It has entered into your world of habits; it has taken roots. Thirty years is a long time. It has taken roots in your body, in your chemistry; it has spread all over. It is not just a question of your head deciding; your head cannot do anything. The head is impotent; it can start things, but it cannot stop them so easily. Once you have started and once you have practiced so long, you are a great yogi—thirty years practicing smoking! It has become autonomous; you will have to de-automatize it." He said, "What do you mean by de-automatization?"

And that's what meditation is all about—de-automatization.

I said, "You do one thing: forget about stopping. There is no need either. For thirty years you have smoked and lived; of course it was a suffering but you have become accustomed to that, too. And what does it matter if you die a few hours earlier than you would have died without smoking? What are you going to do here? What have you done? So what is the point—whether you die Monday or Tuesday or Sunday, this year, that year—what does it matter?"

He said, "Yes, that is true, it doesn't matter."

Then I said, "Forget about it; we are not going to stop it at all. Rather, we are going to understand it. So next time, you make it a meditation."

He said, "Meditation out of smoking?"

I said, "Yes. If Zen people can make a meditation out of drinking tea and can make it a ceremony, why not? Smoking can be a beautiful meditation."

He looked thrilled. He said, "What are you saying?" He became alive! He said, "Meditation? Just tell me—I can't wait!"

I gave him the meditation. I said, "Do one thing. When you are taking the packet of cigarettes out of your pocket, move slowly. Enjoy it; there is no hurry. Be conscious, alert, aware; take it out slowly, with full awareness. Then take the cigarette out of the packet with full awareness, slowly—not the old hurried way, unconscious way, mechanical way. Then start tapping the cigarette on your packet—but very alertly. Listen to the sound, just as Zen people do when the samovar starts singing and the tea starts boiling . . . and the aroma. Then smell the cigarette and the beauty of it . . ."

He said, "What are you saying? The beauty?"

"Yes, it is beautiful. Tobacco is as divine as anything. Smell it; it is God's smell."

He looked a little surprised. He said, "What! Are you joking?"

"No, I am not joking."

Even when I joke, I don't joke. I am very serious.

"Then put it in your mouth, with full awareness; light it with full awareness. Enjoy every act, every small act, and divide it into as many small acts as possible, so you can become more and more aware.

"Then have the first puff: God in the form of smoke. Hindus say, 'Annam Brahm'—'Food is God'. Why not smoke? All is God. Fill your lungs deeply—this is a pranayama. I am giving you the new yoga for the new age! Then release the smoke, relax, another puff—and go very slowly.

> "If you can do it, you will be surprised; soon you will see the whole stupidity of it. Not because others have said it is stupid, not because others have said it is bad. You will see it. And the seeing will not just be intellectual. It will be from your total being; it will be a vision of your totality. And then one day, if it drops, it drops; if it continues, it continues. You need not worry about it."
>
> After three months, he came and said, "But it dropped."
>
> "Now," I said, "try it on other things too."

Clearly, this is very similar to the enlightenment process. One of the differences is that Osho says the mind is powerless. When we think we are going to quit but then don't, we can understand his meaning. However, we know that the mind is very powerful when consistently imbued with joy.

Osho suggests becoming aware of every movement in the smoking process, assuming that awareness is what will free the smoker. We suggest that the essence of awareness is joy. As you allow yourself to enjoy every movement, your awareness expands, and you are free. The distinctions are perhaps slight, but important.

The Last Step

In Step Seven, you forget to smoke, and this might happen at any point along the way. To decide to forget to smoke is a *conscious* choice. You now know what it takes to play with your thoughts, to enjoy them, to move your thoughts away from one focus into another—to forget one focus and move to another. You can consciously forget to smoke whenever you choose. Unlike "Osho's

Smoking Meditation," in the enlightened approach it is not a question of "maybe it will work, maybe it won't." You have the power *now* to forget your smoking habit when you are ready and happy to do so. You are *not* obligated to quit smoking until you are happy to do so. With the techniques outlined in this book, you can choose to do so at any time.

And Now What?

You have now reached a point, here in the book and with your smoking, where you can simply choose to enjoy what you have read, to enjoy where you have been, and to enjoy where you are going. You don't need to make it any more complicated than that. You don't need to analyze what is right, what is wrong, what is helpful, what is not—you simply need to enjoy who you are right now: *your* thoughts, *your* future, and *your* past. Just enjoy!

There is a nice prayer that you might choose to say: "Father, please guide me. You know what I can do, and what I can't do. I will do what I can and leave the rest in your hands."

In the days and weeks ahead, you will discover that you have a greater awareness of your smoking. You will discover that energies are moving that haven't moved in many years. You will recognize that you are *consciously* choosing to smoke and not to smoke; *consciously* choosing to put out your cigarette—though it may be only half-smoked—when you no longer enjoy it. Sure, you might resist these changes or ignore them; pretend they are only temporary. Think that way, and sure enough—that's what they'll be.

Or, you might determine that this is a practical approach—a convenient doorway—through which you can move into a land you've been wanting to explore for a long time. You can use this new energy to propel you into the next stage of enlightenment. The smoker who enjoys all of his thoughts, all of her thoughts, is a brave smoker. You have done it before—you have been this brave before—you can do it again.

Enlightenment is a way of life. It begins when you begin enjoying your thoughts. It is ongoing and never ends. It gets deeper, broader, and more refined.

I think that you'll agree that, once you find enlightenment (joy!), you will never abandon it. It will be your companion all the days of your life.

Isn't that the type of fire you've been waiting to inhale?

Afterword

We encourage all of our readers to write to us at:

The Smokers' Freedom School
606 Hanna Street
Fort Collins, CO 80521

Tell us about your experiences. Whether you've quit or not is not the story we are most interested in, though of course we are pleased to hear such happy news. More importantly, we want to hear about the joy in your life and what it does for you. Have you tried the Enlightenment Exercise? Or your form of it? What happened when you used it in your work life? Your family life? In your relationships with your friends? Your children? Your spouse? How did your happiness affect you physically?

It is in our ordinary daily lives that the Light, the Christ, the Joy, the Immanuel appears. We would love to hear your story.

Notes

Introduction

page ix   Since my first meeting with Dr. Almayrac, I have been fortunate to have had numerous conversations with him as well as to attend many of his public presentations and listen to tapes he has prepared. The quotations from and paraphrases of his talks come from a variety of these sources. I am deeply indebted to Dr. Almayrac for granting permission to include this material in this book.

Chapter 1

page 3   Quote from Deepak Chopra's *Magical Mind, Magical Body* tape series (New York: Nightingale-Conant, 1990).

Chapter 2

page 23   Quote from Chopra, *Magical Mind, Magical Body.*

page 27   Quote from Paramahansa Yogananda's *Autobiography of a Yogi* (Los Angeles: Self Realization Fellowship, 1974).

pages 35–36   Fourteen ways of changing the visual appearance of a thought adapted from Richard Bandler's *Using Your Brain—For a Change* (Moab, Utah: Real People Press, 1985).

Chapter 3

page 39   David G. Myers quote from his *Who Is Happy and Why* (New York: Morrow, 1992).

pages 40–41   Carlos Castaneda's books have contributed much to contemporary American understanding of alternative approaches to spirituality. Among his books are *The Teachings of Don Juan: A Yaqui Way of Knowledge; The Power of Silence; A Separate Reality; The Eagle's Gift; Second Ring of Fire; The Art of Dreaming;* and *Fire from Within.* The quotation on page 41 is from *Journey to Ixtlan* (New York: Simon and Schuster, 1972).

Chapter 4

page 59   G. L. Hemminger's poem is reprinted in *How to Stop Smoking in Three Days,* by Sidney Petrie (New York: Warner, 1979).

pages 59–60   Quote from M. A. H. Russell from *Nicotine Psychopharmacology: Molecular, Cellular, and Behavioural Aspects.* S. Wonnacott, M. A. H. Russell, and I. P. Stolerman, eds. Oxford and New York: Oxford University Press, 1990.

page 63   "Cigarette smoking is probably the most addictive and dependence-producing behavior known to man," from David Krogh's *The Artificial Passion* (New York: W. H. Freeman, 1991).

page 71   Earnie Larson's four criteria from his cassette series *The Transformed Self* (New York: Nightingale-Conant, 1991).

Chapter 5

page 75   The Arica Foundation is located at Dobbs Ferry, New York.

page 81   Song lyrics from "Heart," from the musical *Damn Yankees;* music and lyrics by Richard Adler and Jerry Ross.

page 87   Chopra quote from his *The Path to Love: Renewing the Power of Spirit in Your Life* (New York: Harmony Books, 1997).

page 89   William James quote from *The Varieties of Religious Experience* (New York: Triumph Books, 1991).

Chapter 6

pages 91–92   Yogananda, *Autobiography of a Yogi.*

page 94   Dialogue between Dr. Almayrac and drug addict reprinted from Taped Discussion #4 (available through One Heart Press, St. Louis, Missouri).

page 96   University of Ottawa study cited in "You Can Quit," a pamphlet published in 1993 by the American Cancer Society.

page 97   Mark Twain quote in *Mark My Words: Mark Twain on Writing,* Mark Dawidziak, ed. (New York: St. Martin's, 1996).

Chapter 8

page 112   Lao Tzu in *Tao Te Ching.*

Chapter 9

page 117   Story told by Jack Canfield and Mark Hansen in their *Chicken Soup for the Soul: 101 Stories to Open the Heart and Rekindle the Spirit* (Deerfield Beach, Fl.: Health Communications, 1993).

page 119–20   Forgiveness and healing discussed by Raymond Moody in his *Coming Back: True Tales of Reincarnation* (New York: Bantam,

1992); Leonard Orr and Sondra Ray in their *Rebirthing in the New Age* (Berkeley, Cal.: Celestial Arts, 1983); and Louise Hay in *You Can Heal Your Life* (Santa Monica, Cal.: Hay House, 1987).

Chapter 10
page 134   Quote from Chopra, *Magical Mind, Magical Body.*

Chapter 11
page 142   This chapter title is a respectful reference to Paul Simon's hit song "Fifty Ways to Leave Your Lover."

Chapter 12
pages 147 ff.   References to and quotes from Charles F. Wetherall's ideas and writing are derived from the fourth edition of his book *Quit: Read This Book and Stop Smoking* (Philadelphia: Running Press, 1988).

Chapter 13
page 163–64   Bo Lozoff on fear from his *Just Another Spiritual Book* (Durham, N.C.: Human Kindness Foundation, 1988).

Chapter 15
page 185   Bhagavad Gita text from Sri Krishna Prem's *The Yoga of the Bhagavat Gita* (Baltimore: Penguin, 1973).
page 186–87   Quotations from Yogananda, *Autobiography of a Yogi;* and B. K. S. Iyengar's *Light on Yoga* (New York: Schocken Books, 1979).
page 188   Yogananda, *Autobiography of a Yogi.*

Chapter 17
page 204   Quote from D. T. Suzuki, *Zen Buddhism: Selected Writings of D. T. Suzuki.* William Barrett, ed. (Garden City, N.Y.: Doubleday, 1956).

Chapter 16
page 210   See Hugh Prather's *Notes on How to Live in the World and Still Be Happy* (Garden City, N.Y.: Doubleday, 1986).
page 212   Quote from Chopra, *Magical Mind, Magical Body.*
pages 212–13   Sondra Ray quote from *The Only Diet There Is* (Berkeley, Cal.: Celestial Arts, 1981).

page 213   St. Therese Neumann's fasting described by Albert P. Schimberg in *The Story of Therese Neumann* (Milwaukee: Bruce Pub., 1947).

Chapter 19

page 223   Emmet Fox quote from his *The Power of Constructive Thinking* (New York: Harper and Row, 1979).

Chapter 20

pages 233–36   "Osho's Smoking Meditation" reprinted from Osho's *Meditation: The First and Last Freedom* (New York: St. Martin's Press, 1996). Reprinted by permission of the author.

About the Author

Bear Jack Gebhardt, a twenty-year smoker, is one of the nation's leading stop smoking coaches. He has studied and trained in most of the contemporary addiction-treatment models, and explored many alternative approaches. After studying with the French physician, Christian Almayrac (better known as "Dr. Happiness"), Gebhardt "awakened" to a revolutionary understanding of addiction and smoking. He founded The Smoker's Freedom School (www.enlightenedsmoker.com) to help smokers, their families, and professionals in the field. He lives in Colorado, where he works as a stop smoking coach. He is married with two grown children.